Religion Education And Life

Infant assembly book

Sandra Palmer and Elizabeth Breuilly

CollinsEducational

An imprint of HarperCollinsPublishers

ISBN 0 00 312001 5

First published 1992 by Collins Educational,
London and Glasgow. A division of HarperCollins Publishers.

Reprinted 1993

© Sandra Palmer and Elizabeth Breuilly 1992
The authors assert the moral right to be identified as the authors of this work.

Design by Derek Lee
Cover design by Leigh Hurlock
Cover artwork by Alice Bradbury

Typeset in Great Britain by Saxon Printing Ltd, Derby
Printed and bound by Butler & Tanner Ltd, Frome, Somerset

CONTENTS

INTRODUCTION

Someone once said that schools collect and use assembly books in the way that many cooks collect and use recipe books. The analogy between assemblies and food is in many ways an appropriate one for it is a common thread in many faiths that worship and eating are linked together. In Christianity, after all, the central ritual, that of the Eucharist or Communion, is built around the sharing of bread and wine.

We eat to gain sustenance, to survive physically. It is the religious argument that we also need spiritual sustenance to survive. Jesus and other religious teachers gave spiritual sustenance by making people think and question and reflect on their own way of living and seeing. Many of the assemblies in this collection are designed in a simple and gentle way to help children reflect. They are something to think about.

Building a Community
But eating is also often a communal act. Eating with someone is a means of getting to know them and of gaining a sense of being one with them, of being a community. In the words of the Church of England Communion rite, 'We are one body, because we share in the one bread'. The 'Desert Island' assembly has the specific objective of helping children get to know as people, rather than functionaries, those in the school with whom they have little or irregular contact or little opportunity just to chat to. However, the notion of being a community, and valuing the individuals who make up the community, is a thread throughout the book. The communal acts of silence, singing etc. also contribute to developing this sense of community, as does the singing of 'Happy Birthday' or stopping for a moment to think about those who are ill. Also many of the topics for classroom work in the REAL Infant Handbook lend themselves to being the basis of a class assembly in which the objective is for the school to get to know a particular class and what it has been doing.

Some of these assemblies are concerned with the celebration of things we have in common as a community, whether it be celebrating the beginning of the school year, or remembering together some amusing incident that happened in school, as we suggest in the assembly on 'Laughter'. However we have not presented the use of festival material from different faiths as celebrations because we believe that you can only celebrate something which is yours, which you believe in. Instead we have looked for an idea within the festival which the children could either reflect on or genuinely celebrate. Nevertheless where there are substantial numbers of children of that faith in the school these assemblies could be adapted to be celebrations.

Assembly Focus
Some of these assemblies are described as an assembly focus. They form the core of the assembly and can be slotted into the order of any assembly. One could describe them as 'main dishes', rather than as complete menus. We suggest that you complete the 'meal' with 'side dishes' such as a time to pause and think about the children and members of staff who are sick, perhaps naming those who have a serious illness. Similarly an assembly focus can include sharing the news of the school. Congratulations can be given to the dinner lady who has a new grandchild, the child with a new baby sister, the child who has passed a music exam, etc. and also good wishes can be given to those who are setting off on a new venture whether it be an individual child or a class going on a school trip.

1

Liturgies

Just as some meals have a more formal structure, such as those on important occasions, or Sunday dinner for the whole family, and the menu is carefully planned as a whole, so some of the assemblies in this book are liturgies for particular occasions and are self contained, for example those for Advent, Easter and Remembrance Day. The ideas behind these assemblies will probably be familiar to both you and the children, and that is all to the good. What we are offering new is a way of weaving the ideas into ceremony and celebration. These are not designed to be 'something to think about', but to be an emotional, sensory and spiritual experience.

Just as the formal and festive laying of a table may be an important part in setting the tone of the meal, we feel that the setting of an assembly is important. The surroundings help contribute to the idea that this is an act of worship, not simply a large lesson. Flowers, a picture or an interesting object can transform in a small way a drab assembly hall into a place of reflection – a technique often used by congregations who are having to meet for worship in a bare hall for some reason. Churches and houses are often dressed for special occasions, so we have made some suggestions on dressing the hall for special assemblies.

We suggest, wherever numbers and space permit, that children sit for assemblies in a circle or three-quarter circle as this can enhance the sense of community. Use the space available to you in other ways too, where possible using procession and other movement.

Elements and ideas from the liturgical assemblies given could be used to build a liturgy for any particular occasion that arises. For example, from time to time it does happen that a child or someone in the school dies. In the REAL Junior Assembly book there is one model for a memorial service, which you could adapt. Material from the assembly focus in this book called Remembering our Pet, could furnish ideas to adapt for a memorial service. At the very minimum we suggest that you light a candle to remember the person's life and ask the children to sit or stand for a short period of silence, and that the rest of the assembly should be brief and solemn in tone.

Christianity and other beliefs

In line with the Education Reform Act these assemblies are all Christian in character, in that they are rooted in Christian values, faith, hope and love: faith that each individual is of worth; faith that the world is basically good, though tarnished by humanity's thoughtlessness and greed; faith that life is worth living; hope that good can overcome evil; hope that the act of an individual can make contribution to the whole; hope that even the saddest situation can be redeemed; love of friend, neighbour and stranger; love which is patient and kind, affirming the individual without being boastful; love which sacrifices its own wants for the good of others.

These values are of course shared by many who are not Christian.

The assemblies also draw on Christian forms of worship – the use of music, processions, artefacts, food, notices, preaching/teaching and prayer.

However, they are not centered specifically on God or on Jesus, except in relation to Christian festivals. We believe that this is only appropriate to a community which shares a common religious faith. It is not just that many schools have children from other faiths: for the majority of faiths, worship of a creator/sustainer God would be appropiate. But many schools have substantial numbers of children who are from agnostic and atheistic homes. We believe it inappropriate in the secular school context to presume a common belief in a personal God. Therefore we have made our prayers times of reflection which could be joined in by someone of any religious persuasion or none. In all cases they could easily be adapted to be more specifically Christian or theistic. For the same reason where possible we have suggested hymns and songs in which the theistic language is minimal, and which are joyful, reflective or tell a story.

We have also drawn on sources from other faiths as the Education Act allows and as Christian preachers have done since the beginning of the faith.

Timing

All these assemblies are designed to take about 20 minutes once elements such as singing, school news etc. are included. The actual length will depend very much on your own style of presentation and the degree of response you ask for, and get, from the children. Where a story is included we have given as a guide the time taken to read it fairly slowly, but this again will depend on you.

Other Assemblies
Several topics in the REAL Infant Handbook give suggestions for assemblies specifically related to those topics, usually to be presented by classes at the end of studying a particular topic.

Finally
We hope that just as each cook tends to have a favourite recipe book which is much thumbed from constant use, so this assembly book will soon acquire the same well-worn look. And just as a cook, once familiar with a recipe, will adapt it according to the ingredients she has and the taste of her family, we hope these ideas will help you to build assemblies suited to your own school situation. Happy cooking, and enjoy your meal!

CELEBRATING THE PERSON

Purpose

This assembly is intended to be repeated several times during the year with different guests, so that the children become familiar with the formula. The objective is for children to become aware of members of both teaching and ancillary staff as individuals rather than functionaries. The guest list over the year could include caretaking staff, peripatetic music teachers, and the school secretary as well as teachers.

The topics 'Myself' and 'People' in the REAL Infant Handbook are closely related to this theme.

Preparation

Guest prepares music and other items, and subjects for prayer. Guest and leader discuss the format of the interview.

Resources

Pictures of the tropics and of an island if possible. Other resources as decided by the guests (see below).

Desert Island Discs

Leader: Today we are playing a game. We are pretending that a fierce pirate has sent Mrs ___ to an island in the middle of the ocean. There's plenty to eat there, fruit growing on the trees and chickens which lay eggs to cook. But he has allowed her to take with her a few things – her favourite tape to listen to, and a machine to play it on, some of her favourite food to eat, a photo, her favourite piece of clothing, and a special treat.

Leader then introduces the guest by questioning whether she has ever been to an island before, whether she likes being alone, and whether she is any good at looking after herself.

Leader then asks about each item in turn encouraging the guest to tell a story or explain why the item is special.

Leader asks what the guest would miss least about being at home and what she would miss most.

Prayer/reflection

Leader asks the guest if there is anybody or anything she would like the children to think or pray about. Since this is a personal choice it can relate specifically to the guest's own beliefs and need not avoid references to God, Jesus, Krishna etc. as we have attempted to do elsewhere in this book.

The hymn can be the guest's favourite.

Finally ask her whether she would actively seek being rescued, and how. Ask all the children to wave in the air pretending to be signalling for help for her.

Play the guest's favourite music again for the children to listen to as they leave.

THE SCHOOL COMMUNITY

Purpose
This is intended to be a practical but light-hearted way of drawing out the links which bind people into a community.

Resources
A large ball of coloured wool.

Have the children sitting in a circle, perhaps three deep. Introduce the idea that the school is a community of many people with many different links to each other. Produce a large ball of brightly-coloured wool, and start with the class nearest you. Ask if any child in that class has a brother or sister in another class. Give that child the end of the wool, then unwind the ball and pass it to the brother or sister. In that class, ask for another link, and keep passing the wool around until the whole school is well and truly 'tied up', or you run out of wool!
Some possible connections are:
Siblings
Other relatives
Living in the same street
Sharing the same childminder
Going to the same dancing class
Which class do you go to to borrow a stapler or some scissors?
Which teacher plays the piano if your class is singing?

Does your class join with another class for any activities?
You will know of other connections yourself.
Finally, if you have enough wool left, you could take the wool right round the outside of the circle to symbolise the whole school being bound together as a community.

Prayer/reflection
We are many people;
We are one school;
We are (name of school);
We give thanks for all the different ways that we are linked together.

Classroom links
One class could produce a school newspaper with news of both school events and family news of school members. Children could produce a school "coat of arms" or think up a school motto.

Songs

Come and Praise	19	He's got the whole world (adapt the words to suit the links you have highlighted)
	67	The ink is black
Alleluya	38	With a little help from my friends
	60	A better world.

TIDDALIK THE BULLFROG

Purpose

The theme of the emotions is explored in more detail in the topic on 'Myself' in the REAL Infant Handbook.

This theme is taken up again in the REAL Junior Assembly Book, where the idea that laughing at people can be painful is introduced.

Preparation

Find a good joke, or prepare a funny act, or recall an amusing occasion.

Resources

A large box with a slit in it, decorated in an appropriate manner to be the joke box (with clown's faces, for example);
a picture of a parched Australian landscape;
a picture of a bullfrog.

Tiddalik

(3-4 mins)

Introduce the theme of laughter by telling a joke, or getting someone to act in a funny way at the beginning of the assembly. Or recall an occasion when there was something to laugh at in school – the visit of an entertainer or theatre group, or a spontaneous incident. Ask the children to think about what it felt like to laugh. Laughing makes you feel good, doesn't it? This is a story about laughter that made everyone feel good.

In Australia there are bullfrogs who can swallow huge amounts of water and store it in their throats. This is an Australian aboriginal story about one of them.

It was very hot and Tiddalik the bullfrog was very thirsty. He drank up the water in the stream but he was still thirsty. He drank up the water in the watering holes but he was still thirsty. He drank up the water in the river but he was still thirsty. He drank up the water in the lakes and the billabongs.

Now he was no longer thirsty and his great throat swelled with water. But all the other animals were thirsty – for what was there left for them to drink? The watering holes were empty. The streams and the rivers were dry and the lakes and billabongs were bowls of damp mud.

And Tiddalik, selfish Tiddalik just sat there.

The animals were glum. What were they to do? Someone, I think it was the spiny anteater, suggested poking him with sharp sticks, but they knew Tiddalik's skin was so leathery he wouldn't feel a thing. And he was so huge from drinking all that water that they felt quite frightened by him.

The kookaburra said, "Let's make him laugh! He'll gurgle out the water and we'll all take a bath!"

What a good idea! Worth a try, anyway, they thought. Soon all the animals were trying to do the funniest comic act in all Australia.

All the animals laughed when the kangaroo tried to jump backwards, and fell over her own tail. All the animals, that is, except Tiddalik.

They all laughed when the koalas rolled about in the dust, all except Tiddalik.

They all laughed at the wombat juggling, all except Tiddalik.

So it went on. If they hadn't been so thirsty it would have been a good show. Everyone laughed but the solemn bullfrog determined to hold onto the water.

Then out from the shadows came the snake. It started to twist and turn, in a wild frenzied dance. Round and round, in and out, slithering, sliding, coiling its body into strange shapes.

Was that a flicker of a smile on Tiddalik's face? Yes it was!

Tiddalik

Words and Music by Eric Maddern with Di Walters and Ross Young
© Eric Maddern 1979.

Tiddlalik was a little green frog,
Spent all day sitting on a log,
In the mornings and the evenings too,
He liked to sing a little song for you.
    It went croak, croak, croak, croak, croak,
    Croak, croak, croak, croak, croak.

Tiddalik was thirsty and dry,
He hadn't had a drink for a long, long time,
So he drank up the rivers, he drank up the streams,
The lakes and waterholes it seems.
    He we gulp, gulp, gulp, gulp, gulp
    Gulp, gulp, gulp, gulp, gulp.

Soon the land was very dry,
The birds and the animals thought they might die,
So they walked across the deserts and the dry creek beds,
They gathered round Tiddalik and altogether said,
    We want a drink, drink, drink, drink, drink,
    Drink, drink, drink, drink, drink.

The Wombat said: "Let's make him laugh,
He'll giggle out the water and we'll all take a bath,"
So they danced and they pranced and they tickled all round,
But all old Tiddalik could do was frown.
    He went frown, frown, frown, frown, frown,
    Frown, frown, frown, frown, frown.

The Kookaburra laughed and the Kangaroo hopped,
The little Koala did the bob-she-bop,
The Emu said: "The splits are fun!"
But landed up sitting on his rum-tum-tum.
    He went ouch, ouch, ouch, ouch, ouch,
    Ouch, ouch, ouch, ouch, ouch.

Still old Tiddalik would not smile,
Even at the antics of the crocodile,
Just when the animals had given up hope,
Along came old Snakey sliding down the slope.
    He went Wheeee! Wheeee! Wheeee! Wheeee!
    Yahoo!

Ol' Snakey did a dance like you've never seen before,
He wiggled and he squiggled and he shook some more,
He turned into a spiral and twisted all around,
And soon Tiddalik started to lose his frown.
    He went ha, ha, ha, ha, ha,
    Ha, ha, ha, ha, ha.

Tiddalik did a big belly laugh,
The animals said: "Here comes our bath!"
As he gushed and he poured they drank and drank,
While poor old Tiddalik shrank and shrank.
   They went splish, splash, splish, splash, splish,
   Splash, splish, splash, splish, splash.

Now Tiddalik is a little green frog,
He spends all day sitting on a log,
In the mornings and the evenings too,
He likes to sing a little song for you.
   It goes croak, croak, croak, croak, croak,
   Croak, croak, croak, croak, croak.

Was that the beginning of a grin on Tiddalik's mouth? Yes it was!

Suddenly the bullfrog roared with laughter and as he laughed the water came tumbling from his mouth. The animals cheered as the water-holes filled up again. They cheered as water bubbled in the streams and poured down the rivers. They cheered even more loudly when the lakes and billabongs overflowed.

Tiddalik laughed and laughed and as he laughed he shrank back to his normal size. The animals danced and sang and drank.

Leader: Let's have three cheers for all the things that make us laugh and feel happy inside.

Classroom links

Start a joke box for children to write and drop in their own jokes or stories of things which made them laugh.

Learn the Tiddalik song from Eric Maddern's music.

Making Tiddalik Laugh – Follow up Assembly

Preparation

Sort through the children's jokes and stories from the joke box, finding acceptable jokes to use in the assembly.

Find a 'volunteer' member of staff to be 'Tiddalik'.

Remind children of the story of Tiddalik, how important it was to make him laugh, and how difficult it was to do.

Leader: Today we have someone in assembly who is in the same state as Tiddalik. Look, Mrs. Smith is all puffed up, and she will not laugh. I'm sure we'd all feel a lot better, and so would she, if she would only laugh.

Luckily, we have just the thing here to help. You have all been putting jokes in the joke box, and there must be something here that will make Mrs. Smith laugh. I wonder how many of your jokes it will take?

Invite the authors of the selected jokes to come and read them out, or read them out yourself. Your 'Tiddalik' volunteer can ham it up as much as you feel appropriate. If he or she accidentally laughs too soon, suggest that a few more jokes are required to make sure she does not go back to being too solemn.

Then ask her how she feels, and reflect generally on how jokes and laughter make you feel.

Applaud the children who read the jokes, and applaud the jokes themselves.

Prayer/reflection

Jokes make us laugh
Laughter makes us feel good.
We have laughed together
May we go on feeling good together.

Songs

Come and Praise	95 Rejoice in the Lord Always
	98 You shall go out with Joy
Alleluya	4 This is the Day
	5 Happiness is

THE WISE TEACHER

Purpose

This is a Hindu story although similar stories exist in other traditions. The theme is that we are all learning all the time, we all have some things to learn and some things to teach.

Raj's Sweet Tooth

(2-3 mins)

Raj liked sweets, of that there was no doubt. He spent every bit of money he had on sweets: his pocket money, the money his grandparents gave him, every last coin went on sweets.

His mother would say, "Raj, please give up sweets. Your teeth are rotting with the sugar. You are not eating your proper meals. Please stop buying them."

But it was no use. Sometimes Raj would promise his mother, but when he walked past the sweet shop on the way home from school it was just too tempting. He really loved sweets, and nothing his mother said or threatened seemed to make any difference.

His mother decided to go and see the wise teacher at the temple. If her son wouldn't listen to her, surely he would listen to and obey the wise teacher, she thought.

"Please sir," she said, "Will you tell my son to stop eating sweets. They are rotting his teeth, and stopping him eating his supper. He won't listen to me but I am sure he will listen to you."

The wise teacher listened patiently and nodded his head in agreement. "Yes, yes, I can see you are right," he said." Sweets are not good. They do rot the teeth and take away the appetite. Bring him to me in a month's time and I will tell him not to eat sweets."

Raj's mother was puzzled by this. "But why can't you tell him today? I could bring him to you this very afternoon. Why wait for a month?" she asked.

"No, I cannot tell him this afternoon," was the reply," You must come back in a month."

A month later Raj and his mother went to see the wise teacher.

"Now Raj," said the wise teacher, "You know that sweets are rotting your teeth. They are stopping you from eating properly, so you are no longer healthy. You should give them up."

Raj nodded his head. Yes, he would give them up.

His mother was pleased but she said to the wise teacher. "Why couldn't you have told him this a month ago? Why wait until now?"

The wise man looked at her "A month ago," he said, "I ate many sweets throughout the day. My teeth were rotting and I had no appetite for my proper food. How could I tell your son not to eat sweets when I was doing it myself? No, first I had to give sweets up. Then I could tell him to stop."

Did Raj obey the wise teacher or did he still slip into the shop and buy sweets on the way home? I do not know.

Prayer/reflection

We are all teachers and learners. We all have something to teach others, and something to learn from others. Let us always remember that what we do, and what we see others do, is as important as what we say and what we hear.

HAPPY MEMORIES

Purpose

For the young to appreciate the old and value the past.

Preparation:

Find a photo which has a happy association for you. Ask other members of staff to have ready a "happy memory".

Great-grandma's Memories

(5 mins)

Mrs Brown stood at the bottom of the stairs and yelled, "Steve, Steve, come on! It's time to go. We're late already!"

"Aw! Do I have to come, Mum? It's so boring visiting great-grandma. Why can't I just stay here? I'll be all right by myself. Promise!"

"Don't be silly! You know I can't leave you on your own. Now get a move on or we'll miss the bus."

Steve walked down the stairs as slowly as he could, pulled on his coat and kicked every possible stone he could on the walk to the bus stop. It wasn't until he got on the bus that he noticed his mother had a parcel under her arm.

"What have you got there, Mum?" he asked. "A box of chocolates?" he added hopefully, knowing his great-grandmother would offer him one.

"No," his mother said, "it's an old photo album. I found it when I was sorting through the stuff we cleared from great-gran's house when she moved into the old people's home. I thought she might like it. It was ever so dusty. I sneezed for a good five minutes after I shook out the pages."

Steve lost interest – only an old photo album. He felt sorry for his great-gran. Her hands and knees were crippled with arthritis and she could hardly move. What fun did she have out of life, sitting cooped up all day?

She was in her room when they arrived, sitting huddled up by the window staring out, her back to the door. "Hello gran," said Steve's mother. No reply.

Mrs Brown tried again, "Hello gran," She shouted. Again there was no reply.

Steve tried another tactic. He tapped the old lady on the shoulder and yelled in her ear. "Hello great-gran. We're here!"

His great-grandmother gave a start. "Oh, you did give me a fright," she said. "Why couldn't you have knocked when you came in? I was just watching that wren building its nest. Back and forth, back and forth it was going. He did make me laugh, he was such a busy little thing. What have you got there, Susan? Why, it's my old photo album! I thought I had lost it."

She opened the worn pages. Steve's curiosity got the better of him and he stood behind her looking over her shoulder.

A photo of a small, solemn girl in a checked dress stared back at him.

"Is that you gran?" he asked. "Yes, it's me," she said and she began to laugh. "Don't I look a serious goody-goody! It must have been the only time I looked like that in my life, but I was nervous. It was the first time I ever had my photo taken. I was ever so proud of it because it was a surprise for my mother. We didn't have many photographs in those days. I arranged it all myself, and didn't I enjoy the secret, booking the photographer; persuading my mother to send me to buy something in town; saving the pennies. It was pouring with rain, that's why my hair looks so straggly. But my mother liked it. She often smiled when she dusted it. A great one for dusting, my mother."

She turned the page of the album. This time not one child, but three rows of children standing in a row all looked back at Steve.

"Is that your school photo?" he asked. In some ways it looked just like his own. Rows of children, some smiling, some with silly expressions on their faces, some looking grim. There were differences of course. There were only girls in this one, and it was in black and white and the clothes were very different.

The old lady laughed again. "Yes it is. Can you find me? I was very happy that day. It was the first time ever I made no mistakes in a spelling test and didn't get kept in for making blots all over my writing book. That teacher looks stern, doesn't she? But she wasn't so bad. Once Doris – she was my best friend – and I wrapped up a dead mouse the cat had brought in and left it on her desk. We thought the teacher would scream with fright but she didn't. She thanked us all kindly and said it would make a nice supper. We didn't believe her of course!"

Steve laughed at that, too.

It was the most enjoyable afternoon he had ever had at his great grandmother's, and it passed very quickly. Each photo had a story with it. Some of them were sad and he could hear her voice change when she spoke of them, but most of them were happy ones. When it was time to go the old lady was still poring over the photos and chuckling to herself. Now Steve had stopped thinking of her as a sad old lady. She was someone who had many happy memories to enjoy and who still enjoyed life.

Leader describes a photo she has in her hand (to be put on display later) which conjures up a happy memory, and invites two or three members of staff to speak briefly about a time when they remember feeling happy. It could be the birth of a child, or simply seeing a lovely view, passing a driving test etc., or something that made them really laugh on television.

Prayer/reflection

Leader asks the children to think about a time when they felt happy but to keep it a secret for the time being.

Half a minute's silence.

We give thanks for the memories which make us smile.

Use happy music, either recorded or played by the children. Perhaps use bells, explaining that ringing bells is a traditional sign of happiness.

Classroom links

Children draw "photos" of a happy memory – even if only from the week before, and write about their "photo".

– children ask parents and adult friends about their happy memories and write or talk about them.

– children bring in photos from home to talk about.

– classroom discussion which acknowledges that not all our memories are happy ones.

More Happy Memories – Follow up Assembly

Preparation

Select some of the children's memory work for focus, preferably using children from different classes.

Assembly

Remind children of the story, and the theme of happy memories.

Then call on children to present their memories, with their pictures or writing. Chat with each child and help them to expand their account.

Alternatively, read from a communal book of memories, made from the children's work.

Prayer/reflection

If possible, make up your own here, based on any common themes in the children's memories, or particular things that stand out in their accounts, for example:

We give thanks for games at the seaside and birthday treats.

We give thanks for Caroline's puppy, and the day that John's uncle came and visited.

Songs

See suggestions given in the assembly on 'Tiddalik'.

THE MONKEY BRIDGE

Purpose

For children to know the value of even the smallest contibution to an effort.

The children will need to be familiar with the story of the Ramayana and its main characters. The story is retold briefly in the REAL book *A Tapestry of Tales*, see also the assembly for Divali in this book.

Remind children of the story of the Ramayana and tell the following story from it.

Every Little Helps

(2 mins)

Prince Rama stood on the cliff top and looked over the ocean. In the distance he could just see the island of Lanka. At last he knew that his wife Sita was a prisoner on that island. But his heart was filled with despair. How could he get his army to the island so they could fight the wicked ten-headed demon Ravana who had captured her? How was he going to take his army of bears and monkeys and lots of other animals across? There was no bridge and he didn't have any boats.

Rama felt terrible. He had searched so long. He had come so far. Was he going to be defeated now by the water?

Then the Ocean spoke to him "Rama," he said. "Rama, I am vast and wide and my heart is vast and wide. Lay rocks on me and I will not let them sink. Build a bridge across me."

Rama and his army set to work at once. Everyone helped. The great bears lumbered forward with their arms filled with rocks. The monkeys scampered to and fro carrying stones to build the bridge. Even the squirrel helped. She carried pebbles in her mouth, one by one, and laid them on the road. One of the monkeys noticed what she was doing and he laughed at her feeble efforts

"Hey, everyone!" he called. "Look at this squirrel! She thinks she's helping but look how little she

is doing!" And the other monkeys joined in his laughter.

But Rama stopped them, and bending down he stroked the squirrel's fur gently. Then he turned to them all and said "Each bit of help is as important as another. Not one of us by ourselves could build this bridge. But all of us together can. This squirrel's efforts are as important as any of yours."

Because Rama was a god, the mark of his fingers where he had stroked the squirrel's back showed up as two dark lines. And that is why, even today, Indian squirrels have two dark lines down their backs.

And so it was that together they built that mighty bridge across the ocean and the army crossed and won back Sita.

Take one or two of the major problems in the world, or in your area, or the school, e.g. environmental issues, litter, noise, or some current fundraising effort. Tell the children about them briefly. Indicate how their small individual efforts can help, e.g. recycling waste, not leaving doors open to waste fuel, picking up one sweet paper from the playground.

Prayer/reflection

Even though our efforts are small, we offer them to help our community and our world. May what we have to offer become part of a much bigger effort as we join together.

Songs

Come and Praise	64	The Wise may bring their Learning
	79	From the Tiny Ant
Alleluya	60	A Better World
	61	One man's Hands (you could adapt the words of this)

Classroom links

Classes adopt one particular area of concern, and look at what they can do. Perhaps they could find out about recycling waste, what products can be collected and how they are reused.

Our Small Pebbles
– Follow up Assembly

Preparation

Classwork for one or more classes (see above). Ask each child in the classes concerned to bring a pebble to school. (The size of the pebble may depend on the number of children taking part. If there are many, the pebbles should be tiny, if few they could be bigger to make a visible display.)

Prepare a table where it can be left in place as a display. At its simplest this could show one or two children's pictures illustrating the story, with a brief written summary. A more ambitious plan would be to make models of the land, the sea, and the island, with lines to show where the bridge should go.

Remind the children of the story of the Monkey Bridge.

One or two children from each class describe the problem they have decided to help with, and explain what they are going to try to do, or are doing. After each one, the class together says:

"We each bring a pebble. Together they will build the bridge."

Then children come up and each place their pebble on the table to make a pile, or to make a bridge between land and island if you have prepared models (see above).

Use the prayer/reflection and the songs given above, perhaps adding references to specific things the children have decided to do.

KAREN'S TREE

Purpose

This story is based on a Jewish tale of a young man questioning an old man on why he bothered to plant trees. The purpose is to encourage the children to value trees.

Resources

Find a large picture of a horse chestnut tree.

Another suitable tree, e.g. oak or beech could be substituted in the story if there is one near the school.

The Story of Karen's Tree

(10 mins)

The best thing about Karen's house was that it backed onto the local park. She didn't have to walk anywhere to get to the park. She didn't have to cross any roads. She could just squeeze through her secret hole in the fence and she was there. From her bedroom window she could see the park stretching on and on as though it was her own garden. She liked the colours of the flowerbeds, she liked to watch the dogs playing, and she liked to watch the big mower going backwards and forwards across the grass.

But best of all she liked the tall horse chestnut tree nearest her house. In the spring she watched for the sticky buds getting bigger and bigger until they unfolded into big leaves. Then, a few weeks later, she loved the way its blossom looked like candles. Now it was autumn there were lots and lots of conkers at the bottom of the tree. The other thing she liked was that the tree was home to all sorts of creatures. From her window Karen could see squirrels scampering along the branches and she knew that owls lived in the tree because she heard their hooting at night. Once her mum had found a hedgehog snuffling around the roots of

the tree and had got Karen out of bed so that she could come and see.

Sometimes when Karen looked out of the window she imagined she was a duchess or even the queen. She would pretend that the park was the grounds of her grand palace and that she owned everything in it. The trees, especially the horse chestnut tree, were her trees. They belonged to her.

One night there was a terrible gale. The rain lashed against the window, and Karen could feel the house shake as the wind hit it. Karen huddled up in bed and drew the bedclothes over her head as the wind roared round and round the houses. She imagined she was in a ship battered by the storm and tried hard to be brave. Then she stopped imagining and thought of the animals in her park. She hoped they were safe – especially the squirrels.

Next morning the storm had ceased and all was still. Karen pulled back the curtains to say good-morning to her park. But something had changed, something was different. What had happened to her tree? She rubbed her eyes and looked again. The tree lay on the grass, in a mess of broken branches, with its roots sticking up in the air.

"Mum, Mum!" she called, tearing down the stairs. "What's happened to my tree?"

"The wind blew it down in the storm," her mother answered. "It's an awful shame, isn't it? There have been storms all over the country and many, many trees have been blown down."

Karen wanted to cry. She didn't mind about the other trees but she did mind about her tree. What would happen to the squirrels and the owls and the other birds? Would they be able to find nests somewhere else?

After breakfast she crawled through the fence and went out to inspect her tree. Other people stood around shaking their heads sorrowfully over the tree, but Karen just knew that she felt the saddest.

A few weeks later men came and chopped and sawed the fallen tree. They stacked branches and logs onto trucks and then drove away. Then there was nothing left but the stump. That was the worst of all.

Soon it was Christmas, and then January. One day in a school assembly Mrs Edwards, the headmistress, asked,

"Do you remember those storms and all the trees falling?"

Some of the children looked puzzled but Karen nodded her head vigorously. Of course she remembered. Every time she looked out of her bedroom window she missed seeing her tree. Mrs Edwards went on,

"The park-keepers want to replace those trees but it's very, very expensive to buy new trees. They have asked us if we will have a collection to help pay for them. They want to put in a new horse chestnut near Karen's house. You'll be pleased, won't you, Karen? I will be sending a note home about it today."

When she got home Karen told her mother and grandmother the good news. "Mum! Guess what, guess what. They are going to put some new trees in the park, but we've got to give money. Please mum, can we, can we? I'll give my pocket money!"

"Hang on, hang on," said her mum, reading Mrs Edwards' note. "Yes, of course we will. I've missed those trees, the big horse chestnut especially."

"And I'll give some money too," said Karen's grandmother. "It's an awful pity those old trees have gone. I remember the horse chestnut being there when I was a girl."

Karen couldn't wait to have her tree back again. She hoped the squirrels and the owl would move back in quickly. Then everything would look just as it had before the storm.

Time went by, and one morning the gardeners came with new trees to plant. Karen went to watch them plant where her chestnut tree had been.

The trees were very young and thin and spindly. They looked very small and slight compared to the old ones, but still Karen knew that small things could grow quickly. Last year the tiny sunflower seeds she planted had shot up until they were taller than she was, in hardly any time at all.

"How long will it be before they are as big as the old ones?" she asked the gardener. "Will they be as big by Christmas?"

"Why, bless you, no!" replied the gardener. "They will take fifty years, or longer, to be that size. Yes, fifty years I reckon. I won't be here to see it."

Karen stood open-mouthed. Fifty years! She couldn't even imagine what fifty years was like. She would be fifty-six then. She would be ancient! She would have moved house. She might even be dead. Fifty years was forever!

She dashed home to her mum for an explanation. Her grandmother was visiting.

"Did you know the new tree would take fifty years to grow as big as before?" Karen demanded crossly.

"Yes, we did," replied her gran. "I certainly won't see it that strong again while I am alive."

"But why did you give the money then, for the new tree? What's the point if you are not going to see it? It was a waste of money," said Karen, in a rage.

Her grandmother said "But I will see it, Karen. I will see it grow. I shall enjoy watching the trees look stronger each time I visit, just like I enjoy watching you get bigger and stronger – even though you do get fed up with me saying, 'Haven't you grown!'

"But most of all, I know that someone a long time ago before I was born planted the trees that fell in the storm. The people who planted your tree probably never saw it fully grown, but they didn't think it was a waste of their time and money. And I wish I could say 'Thank you' to them, because I enjoyed that tree all my life until the storm. I won't see these new trees fully grown but other people and animals will enjoy them in the future."

"Perhaps if you have children, when they grow up they will enjoy them. Perhaps if you're ever a granny your grandchildren will enjoy them and collect conkers from under them. You don't plant chestnut trees for yourself, but for the children of the future. And maybe people in a hundred years time will wish that they could say 'Thank you' to you for helping to plant these new trees."

Karen could not imagine ever being a mummy, let alone a granny. But her granny made her think, and she took an interest in the new trees. When spring came round again she was thrilled to see just a few sticky buds on the little trees, and she watched them open into just a few green leaves. Her mother told her that there wouldn't be any flowers or any conkers until the trees were older.

Trees

Words and music by Eric Maddern © Eric Maddern 1981

Chorus: Trees, they must be made to please
Me and you 'cos there's so much we can do
With trees, tra-la,
Oh come and meet my good friends the trees.

All trees make the air fresh and clean,
They breathe fresh air out so we can breathe it in.
And trees are fun for playing in and having a good time,
The Ash tree's a good one to climb and climb and climb…

Chorus

There are many trees that give us food to eat
Like the Apple and the Plum and Mulberry treat,
But one of the favourites of all kids everywhere
Is a heavily laden tree of ripe, juicy Pears…

Chorus

The old spreading Oak is king of all the trees
It has hollows for the birds to nest and hives for the bees,
It stands in the woodland and flowers in the spring,
It's tall and strong and shady and it's why I like to sing about…

Chorus

And when the evening comes you can hear the gentle breeze
As it rustles and it sings through the leafy tops of trees,
The Silver Birch is standing in the pale moonlight,
The old logs are blazing warming up the chilly night.

Chorus

After a while they became her trees – but in a different way to the way the old tree had been. She enjoyed seeing the young trees change with the seasons, and grow a bit stronger as the year passed. And sometimes she would look out of the window and imagine children of the future playing under the branches in fifty or even a hundred years time, when the tree was fully grown and the squirrels, owls and hedgehogs were once more making it their home.

Prayer/reflection
Leader:
We are blessed by trees – they fill our world with green.
We are blessed by trees – we can play with them and climb them.
We are blessed by trees – they shelter animals and birds.
May those who plant trees be blessed.
Children: Amen

Classroom links
Classes visit local parks and identify the horse chestnut and other long standing trees. Children can paint or draw trees and their leaves.

Develop a class project on creatures which live in trees. This could be reported in a class assembly.

Hold a simple fund-raising event in which the children can easily participate, and use the money to buy a strong sapling to plant in the school grounds.

Trees is also a theme in the REAL Junior Assembly book.

BEING DETECTIVES

Purpose

This assembly introduces thoughts on the intangible side of nature, introducing the idea of the spiritual side of life.

Preparation

Particularly suitable for a windy day. The topic on 'The Wind and Weather' in the REAL Infant Handbook takes this theme further.

Being Detectives

The leader of the assembly asks children to be detectives and work out answers from the given clues.

Imagine this scene: Tiles are lying smashed in the garden; a broken branch of a tree dangles over the footpath; leaves and rubbish are scattered everywhere. What sort of day has it been?

(Answer from children.)

We can't see the wind but we can see where it has been. We can read the clues which have been left behind.

Imagine this scene: The room is empty of people but the table is covered with left-overs of food. There are scraps of ice-cream and jelly left in paper bowls. Several small thin candles are scattered about the tablecloth. The plates and cups have pictures of Postman Pat on them. There's just one slice of cake left. It's covered with icing and there are a few balloons hung on the walls. What do you think has been going on here?

(Answer from children)

We don't have to be at the party to see that there has been one. We can read the clues that have been left behind.

Imagine this scene: The back door is smashed open. All the contents of the drawers are spilt on to the floor. There's a plug for a television and an aeriel for a television but there's no television. The child's moneybox is upside down and empty. What sort of person do you think might have visited this house?

(Answer from children.)

You can often see when a burglar has been even if you can't see the burglar.

You can read the clues which have been left behind.

Imagine this scene: The teacher comes out into the playground and finds lots of children glaring at one another. Two children are crying, one is rubbing a hurt leg. What do you think could have happened here?

(Answer from the children.)

A teacher can tell where there's been a quarrel or a fight even if she hasn't seen it. She reads the clues that have been left behind.

Now here is something to think about. How could you tell that something happy had happened in a place? Or that a kind and gentle person had been there? I wonder what clues would be left behind?

Think about what sort of clues you leave behind.

Prayer/reflection

May we always leave good and happy clues behind us wherever we go.

GOOD BUT CAN HARM US

While safety is inevitably a sub-theme of the following assembly, the objective is to help children acknowledge the ambivalence of many things in life by using concrete examples at this infant stage. It is a theme which is taken up in a more abstract way at junior stage.

Resources
Selection of objects: sharp knife; potato; glass bottle; electric kettle; picture or model of car; an iron; a pair of sharp scissors; a hammer; a bottle of medicine; a plastic bag; etc.

Good But Can Harm Us

Take a sharp knife and proclaim it as a dangerous object to the children, asking them to say why it is dangerous.

Then try to chop a potato with a blunt knife and with a sharp one, making the point that sharp things may be dangerous but they are also necessary.

Take a glass bottle and ask the children why they need to be careful with it. When and why can glass be dangerous?

Then ask them to think about why we have glass and what is it good for.

Show them an electric kettle. Ask them why we have to be careful using it.

Then ask them why it is useful.

Look at a picture of a car or show them a model car. Ask them why cars are dangerous.

Then ask them why cars are useful.

Leader: There are many things in this world which are useful and make our lives easier but which can also be dangerous.

Prayer/reflection
May we enjoy the benefits of the many good things around us but may we use them carefully and wisely so that we don't harm ourselves or others.

The assemblies called Fire and Rain take up a similar theme of ambivalence.

FIRE

Purpose
For children to value fire but appreciate that it is also dangerous.

Resources
A box of matches; a large map on which Australia can clearly be seen; a picture of the Australian bush and/or bushfire.

The Gift of Fire – Assembly Focus

(4 mins)

Sometimes we take heat and warmth from fire for granted. But what must it be like without fire? Our food would be raw and tough. We would be cold during the winter months, and we would have no light at night. Today we can make heat from electricity and by lighting gas fires. But these use fire to make them. If we didn't have fire we couldn't have electric lights, or cars, or televisions.

Long ago in Australia the people who lived there knew only too well the importance of fire. They made fires to cook their food, and they used flaming fires at night to guide them. Although Australia is a hot country, especially in the north, at night it can be very cold when the sun's warm rays no longer heat the earth. At night the people sat huddled by the fire. These first Australians didn't have matches but they were skilful at twirling one stick against another until it became hot and set off a spark. They believed that the fire lived in these special firesticks.

As they sat around the fire in the evening, they told each other stories about how people first got fire. This is one of them:

Long, long ago no-one knew the secret of fire-making. No-one could make fire. No-one but the two friends Koorambin and Pandawinda. Selfishly they kept the secret to themselves. Everyone else tore at the food with their teeth, while Koorambin and Pandawinda made their meat tender to eat. Everyone else shivered with cold when the sun went down below the horizon, but Koorambin and Pandawinda stayed warm. Everyone else felt frightened by the great darkness which covered the earth at the close of each day, but Koorambin and Pandawinda had the light from the fire to see by.

The people pleaded with Koorambin and Pandawinda to part with a spark of fire but they would not give it. Some people tried to steal the fire from them but their attempts failed.

One day Koorambin and Pandawinda had built a fire on a river bank. High in the sky the eagle saw the smoke rising, and he decided to help the people obtain the fire. Using his magic powers he made a strong wind which blew among the flames. A spark jumped from the fire into some dry weeds which immediately caught alight. Koorambin and Pandawinda saw what was happening. They desperately tried to put out the fire, but it was no use. The eagle used his magic powers again to stir up a whirlwind. It blew the fire in all directions. The trees on the river bank caught fire, the trees on the great plains caught fire. Soon a great bush fire was raging day and night until the wind died down and it at last burnt out.

Nothing remained, not a tree stood. But the people had caught the sparks of fire and kept them in their firesticks. Now they could cook their food, and warm themselves. Now they had a way of seeing in the dark. But they remembered the devastation and destruction that the fire had caused. They remembered the animals fleeing in terror. They remembered the black and smoking trees. And they remembered the roaring flames. So they used the fire carefully and guarded it. And they told this story to remind their children and their children's children that fire is good but it is also dangerous.

Today fire is still good. And it is still dangerous. It can burn down people's homes. It can destroy woods and forests – the homes of many animals. And of course it can harm animals and people.

Prayer/reflection

Fire is strong – it cooks our food.
Fire is strong – it can hurt us.
Fire is strong – it gives us light.
Fire is strong – it can destroy our homes.
Fire is strong – it warms us.
Fire is strong – it destroys the forests.
We are blessed with the gift of fire. May we always use it carefully.

Classroom links

This can be linked with Science projects on the effect of heat on food.

RAIN

Purpose

To help children to be aware that feelings and attitudes may be ambivalent, and to help them value the importance of rain.

This is a particularly suitable assembly for a rainy day or when it hasn't rained for a long time.

Rain Welcome and Unwelcome – Assembly Focus

(5 mins)

"Please don't let it rain," thought Elizabeth, looking up at the darkening sky, "Not today, not when it's my Aunty Sheila's wedding and I am going to be bridesmaid."

"Happy is the bride the sun shines on," thought her grandfather, looking up at the same sky. "Please don't let it rain. Not today, not when my daughter is getting married, not when it hasn't rained for a whole month."

"Please don't let it rain," thought Sheila, "Not today – not the only day of my life that I am going to be a bride."

All day people looked anxiously up at the sky, hoping and praying that the rain would hold off. Where would they take the photographs if it rained? Would all the guests fit into the marquee, a big tent in the garden, if it rained? They had planned for guests to walk around the garden of the little cottage. The bride and bridesmaid would feel the cold and the damp in their beautiful but light summer dresses and their satin shoes would get all spoiled. How annoying if it rained for the first time today after all these weeks. You could see how long it had been by looking across the fields near the village. The grass was dry and parched, a reddish brown colour instead of the usual green. Yes, the rain was needed – but not today!

Two o'clock came. The service was about to begin and it had not rained. The wedding guests fidgeted in their seats waiting for the bride to arrive. A small child ran up and down the seats. The bride's mother kept looking at her watch. Then they were here. The organist struck up The Wedding March. Everyone stood and half turned to look at the beaming bride walking down the aisle holding onto her father's arm. Behind her walked Elizabeth the bridesmaid, clutching her bunch of flowers, trying not to trip over her dress.

To the small child in the back row the wedding seemed to take ages. His mum had to hush him up by popping sweets into his mouth. To Elizabeth standing ever so still behind the bride the service seemed to take ages, especially as she wanted to blow her nose but her hands were full of flowers. But to the bride's mother as she wiped away a tear, seeing her little girl, grown up and getting married, the service seemed to take no time at all and all too soon the bride and groom, the new husband and wife were walking back down the aisle.

Just then there was a sudden clap of thunder, the skies opened and the rain poured down. The bride and groom stopped still at the church door. Should they go out in it or what? They turned. The photographer hustled them to one side and started taking photos inside the church. Fortunately she had a flash on her camera. First a photo of the bride and groom, then the bride's family with the happy couple and the groom's family, and the bride and bridesmaid, and the bride with this friend and that, till all the photos were done. But it was still raining. There was nothing for it but for them to make a dash to the car, Sheila the bride holding onto her veil, her husband trying to shelter her from wind and rain with an umbrella which had blown inside out.

Later that afternoon the wind and rain had eased. The guests, all crammed into the tent, chatted with each other and with the bride and groom. They all seemed to be saying the same thing, "Lovely wedding, pity that it rained". All the guests, that is, but one. Obed was a friend from Africa, from a country called Kenya. He was studying now in England. "Sheila," he called, "Congratulations, you are indeed fortunate. You will have a blessed marriage, for it has rained on you. Blessed are the wedding couple who are rained upon!"

"What do you mean?" asked Sheila.

"Well, in my country," replied Obed, "We look out across the fields and we see the grass withering in the heat and we long for rain. We see the rivers dry and the cattle thirsty and we long for rain. We have to queue up for the little drinking water that is left, and we long for rain. When it rains and we see everything come back to life again, it is a great blessing. So we say that the bride who is rained on is blessed and brings a blessing. I think your country needed the rain also, didn't it? Everything looked brown and thirsty for the rain. I think it is a blessing that it has come, is it not, and it is a blessing on you that it came on you as a bride."

Through the entrance of the marquee Sheila could see the fields in the distance. Yes, they did need the rain. She still wished that it hadn't rained just when she was coming out of the church, but it was nice to think of it as a blessing on her and her marriage.

Prayer/reflection
Happy the bride the sun shines on.
Blessed the bride the rain falls on.
We give thanks for sunshine and dry days.
We give thanks for warmth, and outdoor play and picnics.
And we give thanks too for cool and rainy days.
We give thanks for the rain refreshing the earth, giving life to all green and living things.
Blessed are we in the rain.
Blessed are we in the sun.

Songs

| Come and Praise | 1 | Morning has broken |
| Alleluya | 58 | Raindrops keep falling on my head |

SHORT BUT SWEET

Purpose
To value and celebrate things which give pleasure for a comparatively short time.

Resources
At least three from the following, or similar objects which have been the source of pleasure to the leader, although their life is brief: a bottle of blow bubble mixture; a bunch of flowers; a piece of fruit; a chocolate; a snowball or picture of a snow scene; autumn leaves or picture of an autumn scene; a picture of a butterfly.

Short But Sweet

Selected children blow some of the bubble mixture, leader comments that the bubbles are enjoyable even though they don't last long. Perhaps make a joke along the lines of "It's beautiful – shall we put it in a box and keep it in the classroom?"

Leader talks about each object saying what it has meant to him or her, however brief the life or fleeting the moment; e.g. "Yesterday I watched a butterfly among the roses, or a ladybird crawled across my hand. It went away quickly and I'll probably not see it again but I was fascinated while it lasted." Obviously some things even in this category last longer than others e.g. the duration of an autumn tree in comparison with a bubble.

Prayer/reflection
We give thanks for rainbow bubbles, floating in the air, although they soon burst.

We give thanks for bright butterflies, fluttering in the sun, although they soon die.

We give thanks for shining white snow, glistening and gleaming, although it soon melts.

We give thanks for all lovely things which have a brief life and end quickly.

Classroom links
Read Teddy Robinson and the Beautiful Present by Joan Robinson, Puffin Books.

Watch 'The Snowman' video based on Raymond Briggs' book.

Children could make a picture of something they have enjoyed or loved, that has died or is finished. (This could be the opportunity to talk about pets that have died.)

WE ARE ALL DIFFERENT

This links with the topics Myself and Pattern in the REAL Infant Handbook.

Purpose
To enjoy the diversity in appearances of people in the school.

Preparation
In the classroom children work in friendship pairs to make comparisons on how they differ in appearance, these should be as detailed as possible.

Resources
Large drawing of "a mother" or a large clear photograph;
a number on a piece of card;
a large photo of a herd of sheep – useful but not absolutely necessary.

We Are All Different

Ask the children to imagine what it would be like if all the teachers looked exactly the same – perhaps all like Miss X – and make affectionate jokes appropriate to the person.

Then ask them to imagine what it would be like if all Mums looked exactly alike and wore exactly the same clothes and had exactly the same voice. Here produce a large simple drawing of a stereotyped mother.

As they emerged out of school, how would they tell their mothers apart from the others? Perhaps everyone would have to wear a badge with their name on. But what if more than one person has the same name? Perhaps a number would have to be the answer! Stick the cardboard number to the picture.

Then what would happen if every single child looked exactly the same? How confusing that would be!

Tell the children about sheep. When you first see a flock of sheep, they all seem to look exactly the same and all the lambs seem to look alike. But each mother ewe can recognise her own lambs, and when shepherds used to have a small flock of sheep they got to know each one by name.

Tell them about when English people first went to China. The Chinese people said that all English people looked exactly alike and that you couldn't tell them apart, and the English people said the Chinese people all looked exactly alike and you couldn't tell them apart. Once they got to know each other they learnt how each one was different.

If there is a pair of identical twins in the school whom you have learnt to tell apart, and who could cope with the attention, talk about how you've learnt to tell them apart because of the differences between them.

Ask children who have prepared work beforehand to come out and describe how they differ from their friend.

Prayer/reflection
Let's all give a big clap because we all look different and at the end say 'amen' after me to show you agree.

We are glad we all look different – Amen

We are glad we are good at different things – Amen

We are glad we have different ideas and thoughts – Amen

Song
Come and Praise 67 The ink is black

Classroom links
Everyone in the school (including teachers) paint a self-portrait or have their portrait painted to make a huge collage in the assembly hall.

IN THE DARK

An assembly for the late autumn or winter. This could also be used in connection with Halloween.

Resources
Either bulbs to plant in a pot or a pot with bulbs already in it depending on the time of year.

In The Dark
– Assembly Focus

Introduction: Tell the children that the Bible says that when God made the day and the night, He said "It is good". It is good to have the light and the day and it is good to have the dark and the night. This assembly is about the good things of the dark.

Then draw their attention to the following:
Bulbs and seeds growing in the darkness, buried warm under the ground.

Perhaps plant the bulbs.

Babies growing in the darkness of their mother's womb.

It is hard to get to sleep in the bright light: even if we have a side light we don't want it too bright. We make it dark to enjoy the light of birthday candles. They wouldn't have the same magic without the dark, it is the same with fireworks. Nocturnal animals hide away in the daytime to avoid the bright lights.

We cannot see the stars in the daytime – they only show up in the dark.

Conclusion: although we need the light, and the dark can sometimes be a bit frightening there are lots of good things about the dark.

Prayer/reflection
Let's just shut our eyes and imagine it's still and quiet like the night.

We give thanks for all the good things that happen in the dark.

Sing a quiet, still song.

BLESSINGS

This assembly could be introduced by a variety of stimuli for which the specific Jewish blessing is given: a rainbow; the new moon; some fragrant blossom; rain after a dry spell.

Purpose
The idea is to encourage the children to rejoice at natural phenomena.

Resources
a picture of the new moon, or of a rainbow;
a branch of blossom, or a picture of it;
the words of the appropriate blessing, large enough for the children to read.

Blessings

Talk about whichever focus you are using. Get the children to observe as much as possible about it. Talk about the pleasure it gives. If a class has been studying that particular thing, get them to come and say something about it.

Tell them that in the Jewish faith it is the practice to say a blessing in Hebrew when you see the new moon, or when you see a rainbow, or when you smell fragrant blossom, and for many other things as well.

Read the blessing to the children and invite them to join in with you for a second reading.

The blessings all start with the phrase:

"Blessed are you, O Lord our God, King of all the world", and then continue with the appropriate line:

    who has created the wonderful things of earth and heaven

or who makes sweet-smelling wood and plants

or who made the great sea

or on seeing a thunder storm:
    whose power fills the whole earth

or on first seeing blossoming trees:
who left out nothing in your world, even such lovely things as trees, as good gifts for people.

For the new moon:
You created all space through one word of yours, yes, all the stars through one word you breathed. You gave each one its place and its movements, and they do not change them. They are glad to obey the rule of the One who made them. You told the moon to reappear. Blessed are you, God, who makes each moon-month new!

For the rainbow:
Who always remembers your promise made when Noah saw the rainbow, and will always keep that promise.
(In the story of Noah, God put the rainbow in the sky as a sign that he would never again destroy the creatures on earth.)

Songs
Sing one of the many 'thanksgiving' songs, e.g. Come and Praise nos. 1-20, 30-40.

Classroom links
Study the phases of the moon; and the rainbow colours; also flowers.

Pick up this theme in further assembly work. Say the blessing with the children whenever an assembly coincides with a new moon, or a rainbow has been seen recently.

OLD BUT VALUED

Purpose

The aim of the assembly is for children to think about something old which they value.

Resources

Something old you value, or a picture of someone old that you care about.

Preparation

Ask the children to see if they can remember all the old things mentioned in the story.

Old But Valued

(3-4 mins)

The family were sitting round the kitchen table at breakfast when Mum made her announcement. "It's pouring with rain, wet and miserable. It's a good day to have a clear out especially of all the old stuff around the house. I'm fed up with all the old things cluttering up everywhere."

Emma, John and Kerry groaned. "Not a whole day clearing out. How boring!"

And their grandfather, pulling a long face, said, "Oh dear, oh dear. I'm old. Does this mean I've got to go? I've just got comfortable and I don't know if the rubbish man will have a sack big enough for me."

"Don't be silly, Grandad," said Emma. "Course Mum doesn't mean you. We like having ..." She stopped when she saw her grandfather's grinning face.

"And what about Honey? She's old. Does she have to go?" piped up John. "She's fifteen and that's very old for a dog."

"And Fred's old for a guinea pig," said Emma.

"And what about you, Mum? You're old. I heard you moaning the other day about how old you were getting," added Kerry.

"Enough, enough!" said their mother. "You know perfectly well I didn't mean people and animals. Now upstairs all of you and get on with the job. Clear out all the old things."

An hour later there was a huge pile of toys and books at the top of the stairs.

Kerry rummaged through the pile to see what her brother and sister had thrown out. "Oh, here's my old rabbit!" she cried, tugging loose a rather dirty pink pile of rags. She hugged it close. "I thought I had lost you."

"What's my elephant doing there?" demanded John. "You can't throw him away!"

"No, of course we won't" said his Mum, coming up the stairs. "Now girls, what were you doing throwing away John's Dumbo. You know how much he loves him."

"But Mum, you said put out anything that's old!" wailed the two girls, "And Dumbo's old and tattered. Look at him. He's filthy – yuk!"

"Well yes, he could do with a wash... and what's this – my teddy! I've had that teddy since I was a little girl. Now be sensible, children. You know I didn't mean anything old that was loved."

"In that case, I'm having back those picture books," insisted Emma. "They may be old and I may be able to read but I still like looking at the pictures."

"And I guess we had better not throw out Dad's coin collection," said John.

"I guess you had better not!" said Mum. "Some of those coins are very valuable. They are very old, you know." And she laughed.

In the end only a small pile went in the rubbish and a small pile was given away. They put Dad's coin collection away in a box lined with tissue paper. Mum washed Kerry's rabbit and John's Dumbo. Kerry put her rabbit on the window sill where she could see him as she lay in bed. John put Dumbo under his pillow, because he didn't want everyone to see him, but he wanted to be able to put his hand under the pillow and feel him at night. Mum didn't want to wash her old teddy – he was so old that she was afraid he would fall apart. So she brushed him carefully, wrapped him in a piece of cloth, and put him in the cupboard where she kept her most precious things. Emma put the picture books on her bookshelf beside her favourite stories.

And Grandad sat down to dinner with a big grin on his face.

Ask the children to recount the old things mentioned in the story.

Show the children something you value although it is old and worn.

Prayer/reflection
Close your eyes and think of something that is old but which means a lot to you or to your family. I am thinking about my [object introduced by you]. You say 'Amen' if you feel the same about what you are thinking about.

You are old – I value you. Amen.

You are old – I will keep you as long as I can. Amen.

You are old – I will look after you. Amen.

Classroom links
Topic on Toys and Treasures in the REAL Infant Handbook. Ask the children to draw something old which they treasure.

STEWARDSHIP

Purpose

This assembly is based on the understanding of stewardship found in Islam, Judaism and Christianity.

Pretend to have mislaid your watch and ask a child or adult to lend you theirs.

Then ask a series of questions expecting the answer 'no' from the children, for example,

Can I jump on this watch if I want to?

Could I give it to a baby to play with?

Could I throw it in the bin?

Ask the children why you can't do whatever you like with the watch.

Make explicit the fact that the watch is borrowed and therefore you have to take care of it.

Ask the children then what it is permissible to do with the watch – to use it to tell the time.

Then explain to the children that many people believe that everything on the earth belongs to God. We don't own the land, or the sea. We don't own houses or clothes. Everything belongs to God, but God has lent things to us, to use and to enjoy. We must take care of them so that others can also use them and enjoy them.

Look briefly at some of the things which the children have, which they can use and gain pleasure from, but which they have a responsiblity to take care of.

Classroom links

The children could make instruction sheets about how to care for the things which they have to look after.

Songs

Come and Praise 73 When your father made the world
76 God in his love for us lent us this planet
79 From the tiny ant

BEING ALONE

Purpose

To draw out the two sides of being alone – the value and the loneliness.

Preparation

This could be used to introduce either of the two assemblies outlined below. There are several stories which illustrate the pain of loneliness – for example *Tubby the Tuba*, *The Ugly Duckling*. Use one of these to introduce the idea of being lonely, or talk about some experience of your own: when you first left home, for example. Talk about how unhappy loneliness can make people.

You could use the traditional rhyme:

Here am I, little jumping Joan
When no-one is with me I'm all alone.

Then talk about the idea, introduced in the above rhyme and in *Tubby the Tuba*, that one can 'enjoy one's own company', or be 'one's own best friend'. What do we value in a friend? What do we do with our friends? Can you do some of those things by yourself? Talk about the idea of talking to oneself, as if to a friend. Perhaps tell the children some of the things you 'say to yourself' when you are alone.

Prayer/reflection

We give thanks for friends
We think about those who are lonely.
We are glad we can all be a friend to ourselves.

1. Simon Stylites

This story could be dramatised with children playing the parts, perhaps with 'Simon' climbing higher and higher up a piece of PE apparatus. If possible, point out a nearby building or tree that is 20 metres high, the final height of Simon's pillar.

(5 mins)

Hundreds of years ago there lived a boy called Simon. He was a Christian, and he loved God very much. He loved to sit very quietly and pray, and when he did that, he heard God speaking to him. But it wasn't always easy to be quiet. He tried finding a quiet corner at home, but before long he heard,

"Simon! Simon! Could you cut some wood for me?"

or

"Simon! Simon! If you give me your best coat now, I'll wash it for you."

or

"Simon! Simon! Your aunt has come to visit!"

It wasn't that he didn't want to see his family, or have his coat washed. It was just that he was trying to listen to God. So when Simon was grown up, he decided to join a monastery, where men lived together, prayed together, and listened to God together.

"Now I shall be able to spend all my time listening to God," thought Simon, "with nothing to interrupt me."

But although there was a lot less noise in the monastery, and no-one kept calling "Simon! Simon!", it still wasn't quiet enough to suit Simon. There were bells which rang to tell him when to go into the church, when to eat his meals, when to help with the work, and when to go to bed. And it always seemed to Simon that just as he had become quiet enough to listen to God properly, a bell would ring for him to do something else. He did manage to listen to God some of the time, but for Simon it wasn't enough.

"Part of the trouble," he thought to himself, "is the way we live. We spend a lot of time cooking the food, digging the garden to grow vegetables, weaving wool for our cloaks, sawing wood to make beds, chopping logs to make a fire. If I lived a more simple life, I would have more time to listen to God."

So he left the monastery, and went to live all by himself in a very lonely place. He didn't bother with new clothes, he just wore whatever rags he had. He only ate the berries and nuts that he found, and he didn't light a fire for warmth. At first things were much better. He spent hours listening to God, and the more he listened, the more he loved God, and the wiser he became. But there were still problems. This time it wasn't other people who interrupted him. It wasn't long before Simon heard a strange rumbly voice:

"Simon! Simon! This is your stomach speaking. I've had nothing in me since this morning. When are you going to feed me?"

"Be quiet, stomach," said Simon, "I'll feed you when I've finished listening to God."

Then it was a shivery voice from his back:

"Simon! Simon! This is your backbone speaking. It's cold back here. When are you going to find some more clothes?"

"Be quiet, backbone," said Simon, "I'll get some more clothes when I've finished listening to God."

Then there were two jumpy voices from down below:

"Simon! Simon! These are your feet speaking. We're getting tired of sitting still. When are we going to run around?"

"Be quiet, feet!" said Simon, "I want to sit still and listen to God."

It took a long time before Simon taught all the different bits of himself to be quiet when he was listening to God. Gradually he found he could listen more and more, and he became wiser and wiser. But it wasn't long before people found out that there was a very wise man living in that lonely place, a man who listened to God.

"Simon! Simon!" said a mother who had walked many miles to find him. "My child is sick. Please ask God to make her better."

"Simon! Simon!" said a young man. "I don't know whether I should be a carpenter or a farmer. Please ask God what he wants me to do."

Simon gave the best advice he could to everyone who came to him, and he prayed to God about their problem. The people were grateful for his help, and brought him food and clothes. But the one thing they couldn't give him was enough quiet time on his own to listen to God.

"This is no good," said Simon to himself. "I must find a way to get away from all these people. I cannot help them if I cannot listen to God." So he asked the people to help him build a high tower, with a little platform on the top.

"I will live on top of the tower," said Simon, "and I will let down a basket on a string every now and then. Put some food in the basket, and write down all your problems on a piece of paper. I will pull the basket up, and give you the answers when I have listened to God."

The people gladly helped Simon build the tower, and kept his basket full of food and drink, as well as full of problems. For a while it worked very well. Simon had enough quiet to listen to God, and he was still able to give the people his advice, and tell them what God said. But as time went by, more and more people heard about Simon-up-the-pole, as they called him, and more and more people came to ask his advice. And they were not all willing to wait for his answer.

"Simon! Simon!" they shouted at the bottom of the tower. "Simon! Can you hear me? Why don't you answer me?" And they would jiggle the rope that held his basket, and shout louder and louder, and jump up and down and wave their arms, till Simon found he just couldn't listen to God any more.

"It's no good," he told the people. "We'll just have to build the tower higher."

And so it went on. Every time Simon-up-the-pole built the tower higher, people would come with more and more noise, bigger and bigger crowds, just to hear what Simon had to say. And as the crowds got bigger, so Simon asked people to build his tower higher and higher. People far and wide were talking about Simon-up-the-pole. Kings and emperors came to ask his advice, and everyone who heard him went away knowing that they had heard a very wise man who loved God, and it made them want to listen to God more themselves.

By the time Simon died, an old man, he was living on top of a narrow tower about 20 metres high. And to this day he is known as Simon Stylites, which is Greek for Simon-up-the-pole.

Prayer/reflection

Simon found a place to be alone and quiet.
We think about the places that we can be alone and quiet:
in the quietest room in the house;
at the end of the garden;
in bed at night.
We give thanks for the quiet.
We give thanks that we can sometimes be alone.

2. The Still, Small Voice (1 Kings 19:12)

Preparation

This story could be illustrated by children who have prepared percussion pieces for the wind, earthquake and fire.

(2 mins)

Elijah the prophet lived many thousands of years ago in the land of Israel. He prayed to God, and listened to what God said to him, and then he told the people of Israel what God had said. But very often the people did not listen to him. The King and Queen of Israel did not do what God said. Many terrible things happened in Israel at that time – people were killed, the rain did not fall, the crops did not grow, and people were hungry. The King thought that all this was Elijah's fault, because Elijah kept saying, "You are making God angry". So he sent his soldiers to find Elijah and kill him.

Elijah knew they were coming, and he ran away. He travelled for many days and nights through desert and lonely mountains, until at last he came to Mount Horeb, called 'the mountain of God'. Tired, cold and hungry, Elijah crept into a cave, and there he spent the night. As the night was coming to an end, he heard God speaking to him:

"Elijah," said God, "What are you doing here?"

"I have always been on your side, O God", said Elijah, "I have spoken out for you when all the other people turned their backs on you and did wrong things. I told them they were wrong, and they went on killing the people who were on your side. Now I am the only one left, and they are trying to kill me."

"Go out of the cave and stand on the mountain," said God, "for I am going to come to you."

Now Elijah was partly afraid and partly glad, for he knew that God was very powerful.

"God controls the seas and the earth and the sky," he thought. "God could shake the earth, or flatten this mountain, or send lightning out of the sky. He is angry with my people, the people of Israel. Perhaps he will send a great wave to swallow them up. I have seen the mighty things that God can do, and I am afraid. But God has told me to go and stand on the mountain, so that is what I must do."

As Elijah stepped out, a great blast of wind hit the mountain. The wind roared, Elijah staggered back against the mouth of the cave, and even the rocks were rolled over and cracked apart by the strength of the wind. But as Elijah cowered back against the mountain, he realised that God was not in this great and terrifying wind.

The wind died down, but all was not quiet. From deep in the ground there came a rumbling sound, and Elijah felt movement under his feet. The ground shook, the mountain rocked, as a great earthquake hurled the rocks in all directions. Elijah was terrified, but he knew that God was not in the earthquake.

At last the earth was still, but Elijah could still hear a roaring noise. A roaring and crackling noise that grew louder and louder as a fierce fire swept by him across the mountain. The flames leapt up to the sky, and the smoke swirled round him in clouds, and Elijah could feel the fierce heat of the fire as it rushed past. Elijah pressed back into the cave to get away from the burning heat, but he knew that God was not in the fire.

And then it was quiet. So quiet that Elijah found himself holding his breath to hear the next sound. If God was not in the wind, the earthquake or the fire, what powerful and frightening noises would there be when God himself came? But still it was quiet.

And then Elijah heard it. Elijah could not be sure he heard anything until he held himself absolutely still and quiet. In the quiet, Elijah knew that God was speaking to him. He went out of the cave and stood up, and covered his face with his cloak. God was speaking to him, and he felt both afraid and glad.

Prayer/reflection

Thunder rumbles, traffic rumbles;
The wind rushes by, people rush by;
Fire roars, voices roar.
But when quiet comes
Our minds can be quiet
Let us listen for the still, small voice.

Songs

Come and Praise 60 I listen and I listen
68 Kum ba Yah
96 A Still Small Voice

HOW SHOULD YOU JUDGE OTHER PEOPLE?

Purpose

This story is loosely based on an old Islamic folk tale. It raises the question of how we should judge other people. It may puzzle the children but give them something to think about.

Assembly Focus

Once Hajji arrived home from a long journey to find an invitation to a great feast waiting for him. It was that very night and he didn't have time to change, so off he went in his old, shabby, dirty travelling clothes.

The feast was being held in an enormous tent. Hajji stood in the doorway and looked inside. The room was aglow with lights, and swathes of multicoloured material festooned the tent. Men and women dressed in satin and silk, mink and ermine chatted and laughed. Children played amongst them, joking and teasing each other. Servants bustled about offering sumptuous food. Hajji looked down at his ragged worn clothes. They didn't seem very suitable, he thought, but never mind. He found himself a seat and settled down to enjoy himself.

But did anyone talk to him? No. The adults took one look at his clothes and turned their heads away. Nor did the waiters stop and offer him food and drink. They put their noses in the air and walked on by. Everyone ignored him. It was as though he didn't exist. Hajji had had enough. Off home he went. He changed into spotless garments, clothes that gleamed and sparkled. Now he looked like a prince.

And when he returned to the party he was treated like a prince. People stopped mid-conversation and turned to him. Waiters hurried towards him to offer him food.

Hajji took the drink and he poured it over his trousers. He took the food and he rubbed it into his jacket.

"What are you doing?" cried the children, astonished to see a grown up behave in such a peculiar way. They would get into trouble for doing such a thing. Would he?

"What are you doing?" cried the mothers and fathers, horrified by such behaviour. What an example to set the children!

"What are you doing?" cried the waiters shocked that such a thing could happen at so great a feast.

"I am feeding my suit," replied Hajji. "When I came before you dressed in my tired old travelling clothes, you ignored me and I went home. When I returned in my beautiful clothes you offered me food. I am the same person. The only thing different is my clothes. You must have invited the clothes not me. You didn't offer the food to me. You offered it to my clothes. So I have fed my clothes."

Prayer/reflection

Ask the children to stop and think about the story. Have they ever ignored someone because of the way they were dressed. Then say: Let us learn to treat people according to who they are, not the way they are dressed.

Songs

Come and Praise   88 I was lying in the Roadway
                 97 'Tis the Gift to be Simple
                101 In the Bustle of the City

SAINT KEVIN AND THE BLACKBIRD

Purpose

This story highlights the love of one person for creation and how he acted it out in his own life.

Assembly Focus

Long ago in Ireland, Kevin, a man of God, knelt by the open window of a church. His arms were outstretched, his palms open towards the sky. He was praying, praising God for all creation; for birds singing in the trees, and fish leaping in the streams, for blue skies and dark brooding thunderstorms, for rugged rocks and pleasant meadows. And as he prayed a blackbird swooped in through the window and filled his hand with soft moss. And as he prayed she sat on the moss and laid an egg.

Kevin, in the midst of his prayer, became aware of the soft moss and the extra weight in his hand. He opened his eyes and saw the egg. He saw the blackbird land again on his hand and make herself comfortable. To her Kevin was a tree and his hands the branches of a tree.

Kevin was frightened that he would damage the egg and frighten the blackbird if he moved his hand. So he knelt there, as still as still can be until the blackbird hatched her egg, and the young chick flew away.

Many years later after Kevin had died, he was made a saint because he was such a holy, loving man. And the statues and pictures of him always show him with the blackbird making her nest in his open hand.

Prayer/reflection

May we learn to love and care for creation as Saint Kevin loved and cared for creation.

Classroom links

Ask children to paint a picture of the scene and also to imagine what happened afterwards.

Songs

Choose any from the "Caring for the World" section of Come and Praise.

WHAT MAKES LIFE WORTH LIVING?

Purpose
Sadly, pictures of hungry people in the slum dwellings of cities, or refugee camps fill our television screens all too often. It is easy to forget, though, that life isn't just about keeping the body alive. Poverty means a lack of more than food or shelter. This assembly is to encourage children to reflect on this idea. It is also important to get across the idea that not all Indians are poor.

Resources
A map of the world to show where India is, and possibly some pictures depicting poverty, and Indians who are comfortably off.

Assembly Focus

India is a country with many, many millions of people. Some of the people are very comfortably off with big houses, and motor cars. They eat and live well. Many people in India don't have much money but they have enough for a home, they have enough to eat and to have the occasional treat. But there are many others who have nothing. Some live in makeshift houses made out of other people's rubbish, corrugated cardboard, old packing cases, abandoned cars. Sometimes they have just enough money to buy some rice, perhaps a few vegetables but often not even that. They scavenge in other people's dustbins, they sweep the streets to collect the grains of rice that might have fallen in the dust. After a whole day sweeping and sifting the dust for rice, they might just find enough to make a meal. They often go hungry. They rarely feel as though they have had enough to eat.

A missionary doctor in India was sent some money by a friend in a church back home. "Give this to someone who needs it," the friend had said in the letter.

"I know just the family," thought the doctor. He had seen them the week before; the eldest boy had cut his leg quite badly and the doctor had cleaned the wound and stitched it up. There was no father and the family often went to sleep with hunger gnawing at their stomachs. He sent one of his assistants round with the money to the family, thankful that for once they would be able to buy enough to eat.

A week or two later he saw the mother again.

"Thank you so much for your gift," she said, 'We went to the pictures. We had a wonderful time."

The doctor was astonished. "You went to the pictures!" he said, "I thought you would buy food with it. Your family is always hungry."

"Yes," said the mother, "My family is always hungry. If our stomachs are full today, we will be hungry again tomorrow and the next day and the next day. Some days we may be lucky and have enough to eat. Most days we will not. But we have never been to the pictures before and we will probably never go again. But we will remember it for a very long time. We may be poor but we too need a treat occasionally."

Then the doctor understood, because he knew that he needed treats sometimes too.

Prayer/reflection
Think about the story.

Classroom links
Discuss what the children see as treats.

Song
Alleluya 5 Happiness

MOTHER LOVE

Purpose
This assembly is to encourage children to reflect on ways parents show love.

Resources
A picture of Krishna.

Something to Think About

Ben noticed the black string round Sanjay's neck as they were getting changed for P.E. He was dying to know what it was but he couldn't ask because talking was definitely *not* allowed during P.E. All through the P.E. lesson Ben kept on wondering. In fact he slipped once because he wasn't concentrating.

"What's that funny black thread you've got round your neck?" he asked his friend when it was playtime at last.

Sanjay looked a bit embarrassed. "My Mum wants me to wear it," he said. "She is always worrying about me. She's scared that if she's not with me to look after me all the time, I'll get hurt."

"Yeah, my Mum's like that," said Ben. "If I go to the corner shop, she says, 'Now remember, don't cross any roads, and don't go with a stranger and you had better wear an anorak or you will get wet. And go straight there and come straight back!' Sometimes I get a bit fed up. But what has that got to do with the black thread?"

"Well, my mother prayed to our god Krishna to ask him to protect me especially when she's not around to look after me. She took the black thread and laid it next to Krishna's statue in the temple, and she asked Krishna to bless it. Then she tied it round my neck. Now when I touch it I think of Krishna's love and my mother's love."

Ben thought about Sanjay's Mum putting the thread round his neck. He thought of his Mum putting her arms around him and giving him a big hug. And he thought of his Mum always going on about keeping safe. Maybe they were all ways of showing love, he thought. And then he thought about playing a game of football and ran to join his friends.

Prayer/reflection
We give thanks for the care of those who look after us.
For food and shelter
For keeping us safe
For loving arms around us.

Song
Come and Praise 19 He's got the whole world.

Classroom links
Look at the chapter called Family in the REAL Infant Handbook.

AKBAR

Note: Equality is an important theme of Sikhism. Although this story could be used in isolation where the children have little or no knowledge of Sikhism, some background makes it more interesting. Several topics in the REAL Infant Handbook can introduce children to the Sikh faith. See the 'Introduction to Sikhism' in the Infant Handbook.

The Guru and the Emperor: A Story to Think About

Usually people are very excited if the Queen or a prince wants to visit their home. They clean up the house, sometimes they even get the whole place redecorated because they are so pleased at having such an important guest. And if the Queen invites them to the Palace they don't say, "I'll think about it", or "I am not sure, I'll see what I'm doing". They say "Yes thank you", and go and buy new clothes for such a special occasion.

Several hundred years ago in India there was a great emperor called Akbar. An emperor is even more powerful than a king and in those days emperors were very powerful indeed. If an emperor said something you did it. If he asked to visit your home you flung open the doors and let him come in.

Now Emperor Akbar had heard about a new religion called Sikhism and he had heard about the wisdom of its leader and teacher the Guru. He was filled with curiosity about the Guru. What did he look like? He must be teaching something very interesting if so many people wanted to hear it. He decided that he would like to come and speak with the Guru.

Emperor Akbar sent his messenger to the Guru. "The Emperor wishes to speak with the Guru," the messenger announced.

The Guru looked thoughtful when he heard this message and he sent this message back. "The Emperor may come and speak with me but first he must eat in our big dining hall with anyone who wants to eat there that day."

"Oh, yes" said the messenger, "you'll want to invite some important people to see the Emperor."

"No, I don't mean that", said the Guru. "Every day many different people come to see me – rich and poor, clever and foolish, young and old. All of them sit down together to eat before they see me, for in the sight of God they are all equal. The Emperor must come and sit with them, for in the eyes of God he is no more important than the man who sweeps the road outside."

The messenger took this message to the Emperor.

"Yes, the Guru will speak with you but first you must eat in the big dining room at the Sikh village."

All those at the court looked on with fear and trembling. What would Akbar say? Surely he would be insulted? Would he be angry? The Emperor Akbar was used to clean people in fine clothes. He was used to being with important people who had important jobs. No, no, the courtiers thought to themselves. Akbar would not go and eat in the Sikh dining hall. Why he would not only have to sit and stand next to filthy people. He would have to talk to them!

But the courtiers were wrong. Emperor Akbar said "Yes", to the Guru's invitation. He went to eat in the Sikh dining hall and he ate with the beggars and the ordinary people, the people who were servants, or ploughed in the fields and who did the dirty jobs. Then the Guru spoke with him and told him that all people are equal in the sight of God – a beggar is as important as an emperor, a cleaner is as important as a prince, a man without a single coin is as important as the richest person in the world.

Emperor Akbar did not become a Sikh but many say he was a wise and kind ruler who did treat all people equally. Perhaps he learnt something the day he visited the Guru.

The dining hall where everyone sits down together is still important to Sikhs. Whenever they meet together for a service, they bring food or money and they take it in turns to cook a meal which everyone shares, whether they are Sikhs or not, and whether they are rich or poor.

Note

We suggest you do not ask the children to reflect specifically on this story, as drawing too pointed a moral could be counter-productive. We have therefore not provided a prayer/reflection here. Ask the children to spend a few moments (perhaps 20 seconds) quietly thinking about the story and what it means, but leave them to draw their own conclusions.

Song

Come and Praise 97 Simple gifts

SAYING AMEN

Purpose

The purpose for this assembly is for children to learn what "amen" means, so they understand its use in worship and for children to think about ways of agreeing.

Amen is a Hebrew (originally Aramaic) word which has its origins in Old Testament times but has been used liturgically by the church since its early Greek-speaking days. It means "verily", or "truly", and signifies solemn agreement.

Preparation

Think of suitable items for the "Best of..." list (see below).

Saying Amen

1) Announce to the children that you are going to tell them what you think is the best television programme, the best football team, the best pop group, the best flavoured ice cream, the best toy to play with, etc.

Tell them that if they agree they should nod their heads, vigorously. If they disagree they should shake their heads. If they don't have an opinion they should do neither.

Go through your 'Best of...' list.

2) Then repeat the exercise but this time ask the children to say yes or no if they do or don't agree with the following sorts of statements:

e.g.
Swimming is fun.
Splashing in puddles is fun.
It's lovely when it snows.
Football is fun.

3) Then introduce the word "amen" and ask them where they have heard it before. Tell them that it's a Hebrew word and it means the same as nodding your head or saying 'yes' as the children have just done. But stress it means saying "Yes I truly agree, I agree very, very, very, much !"

So that's why people say amen at the end of prayers. It should show that they truly agree with what has been said.

4) Then ask the children to say "amen" to the following but only if they truly agree with what's been said.

We are glad it will soon be spring, summer etc.

We hope (appropriate names) all have a happy birthday.

We hope (appropiate name of anyone in the school who is ill) will soon get better.

We hope we will do good work today.

Think of other expressions in your own situation which the children will be able to say 'amen' to.

Song

The refrain from Alleluya 77 Amen.

DIVALI

The dates for this Hindu festival vary from year to year but it is usually sometime in October. It is a new year and harvest festival as well as commemorating the restoration of the proper balance between good and evil when the demon king Ravana was defeated by Rama, the god Vishnu in human form. (See notes on Divali and Introduction to Hinduism in REAL Infant handbook.)

The harvest aspect of Divali is part of the assembly for Harvest Festival, where the custom of putting down rangoli patterns made of foodstuffs, so that the animals can share the harvest, is used.

Purpose
This is intended to help children to value festivals from traditions other than their own, and to mark an occasion which is important to a major ethnic group in Britain and to convey the hope that evil need not go on for ever.

Preparation
In the classroom, make rangoli patterns to display round the hall.

If a class is going to act out the story they will obviously need preparing. However many children will also respond to being given the part and following the directions while the story is being told. Masks are a good way of differentiating between the characters.

Resources
Some Indian artefacts or objects, both 'exotic ' and ordinary and everyday, and/or pictures of people in traditional Indian dress. Oxfam shops are full of such goods.

A record or tape of Indian music. Many record shops stock recordings of sitar music.

Play some Indian music for the children as they come in and let them listen to a little more for a while.

Divali

1) Introduction. This will of course vary according to the location of the school and ethnic mix. It could start by looking at the objects from India, commenting that some have a distinctive look, while with others it is hard to tell where they are from. Say that many people in Great Britain had parents or grandparents who came from India although they may have lived in other parts of the world too. Of these people many belong to the Hindu religion which began in India.

Hindus are now celebrating Divali in which they remember the story of how Prince Rama fought the wicked demon Ravana.

2) Children give their performance of the mime of the story of the Ramayana or you can tell the children the story asking them to cheer every time you say Rama and boo every time you say Ravana.

3) Sing or learn a simple Hindu chant or Come and Praise 140, which is based on a Hindu prayer.

4) Lead the children in giving cheers for all that seems good in the world. e.g. kindness, friendship, love.

Then ask them to boo things which seem bad – greed, selfishness, hatred, bullying.

Prayer/reflection
When things seem bad around us give us the courage to stand up for what is right and good and the hope that it will stop and good will come.

Finish the assembly with listening to more of the Indian music.

CHINESE NEW YEAR

Warning This is noisy because Chinese New Year is a noisy celebration. The sense of the festival would not be conveyed without the noise.

This could be an assembly by one class or in which children were drawn from different classes.

For this assembly the children would need to sit in two blocks facing each other so that there is a wide path down the middle and a path at the back of each class. It is an assembly that would be particularly effective in a hall with classrooms off it.

Preparation

Hang red door banners by each classroom door, or give two children from each class the responsibility for holding them.

If the whole school has been studying Chinese New Year then each class can make its own banners, if not the class involved can make door banners for each of the other classes.

Have a blossoming plant in a pot – either real blossom or paper blossom.

Have hanging a large picture painted by the children of the kitchen god.

Resources

Recording of Chinese music. One good example is 'Like Waves Against the Sand', CSDL 325 from Saydisc Records, Chipping Manor, The Chipping, Wotton-under-Edge, Glos., GL12 7AD

Chinese New Year

Listen briefly to Chinese music.

Leader: This week Chinese people all over the world are celebrating Chinese New Year. Let's see what is happening today in assembly. But first let's find out about some of the things in our hall today.

A child explains about the blossom being a sign of good fortune – the hope that good things will happen in the coming year.

Another child talks about the kitchen god. (See REAL Infant Handbook p64.)

Another explains about the door banners. (See REAL Infant Handbook p65.)

Out of sight there are sounds of clashing gongs and children imitating the noise of firecrackers whooshing and cracking.

Leader: What's that noise?

The Chinese lion comes into view accompanied by the loud banging.

Leader to children making all the noise: Stop, stop. What are you doing. Why are you making all that noise ?

Children: We are driving away all the bad fortune so that it doesn't come into the new year.

Leader: What sort of bad fortune?

The children making noise name various events they consider to be bad.

Leader: Now everybody else make the noise to drive away the bad fortune.

Leader to lion: Who are you? What are you doing?

Lion: I am the good luck lion. I am going visit all the classes to bring them good fortune.

Lion weaves its way round the room, either visiting each classroom door or with children making archways. At each stopping place a child reads one good luck wish on the banner. After each visit the rest of the children cheer.

Leader: Let's wave goodbye to the dragon as it leaves the room.

Let's wish all Chinese people everywhere a Happy New Year.

All: A Happy New Year Everyone!

Play Chinese music.

Alternatively have a simple class assembly in which children report on their studies of Chinese New Year or simply use the information in the REAL Infant Handbook to tell the children about Chinese New Year.

RAMADAN

This assembly would be appropriate towards the end of Ramadan, so that the follow-up on Eid is fairly close, and children can watch the moon for themselves, weather permitting.

The Muslim month of Ramadan is a period of fasting during which Muslims do not eat or drink between sunrise and sunset. This is in obedience to a command in the Qur'an. Muslims see it as a period of self-discipline and identification with the poor (these themes are taken up in the topic on Ramadan in the REAL Junior handbook). The Muslim calendar is a lunar one so each year Ramadan is slightly earlier according to a western calendar. During the 1990's it will be in spring. The ill, pregnant women and travellers are exempt from the fast but are expected to make it up another time. Young children are not expected to undertake the full fast, but gradually take on more and more as they get older. See also the topic in the REAL Infant handbook on Eid ul-Fitr.

Purpose
This is meant to mark with the children an important period for many people in this country.

Assembly Focus

Talk with the children about 'How do we know when it's time to…? (e.g. time to get up, time to go to school) Finish with 'How do we know when it is time to plant seeds in the ground?' Tell them the answer – when the ground is warm, or when there is no more frost at night, or when the grass begins to grow. Keen gardeners wait eagerly for these signs.

Muslims are waiting eagerly for a different sign – for the new moon. For when the new moon comes it will tell that the fast of Ramadan is over, and they can eat and drink whenever they want again.

Explain to them that people of the Muslim religion are fasting through the hours of daylight for a month. Tell them about the exemptions from the fast.

When the new moon appeared they knew it was time to start fasting. For the next two weeks, as the moon looks bigger and bigger, they kept fasting, and now they will go on fasting as the moon looks smaller and smaller. Finally the moon will disappear for one night, and Muslims know that when they can see the tiny, thin new moon the next night, it will be time to stop fasting and celebrate with a big festival. In Britain it is often difficult to see the moon because of the clouds in the way, but many Muslims have friends and relatives in countries where there are few clouds in the sky, and they telephone them to find out if the new moon can be seen.

In countries where there are not many clouds, people often wait up all night to see the new moon, and they are very excited and happy when they can see it.

Talk about the many different reasons why people might fast – to lose weight, because of illness, raising money for charity, etc., and emphasize that these are not the Muslim reasons for fasting.

Then tell them that it's because they are obeying the words in their holy book the Qur'an. They believe that God told their prophet Muhammad what to put in the Qur'an, so if they are obeying the Qur'an they are obeying God. They believe that what God tells them to do must be the best for them. Emphasize how hard it is for them to obey, especially in hot countries.

Prayer/reflection
Let's think about Muslims everywhere and hope that they will be well and strong enough to keep to their fast.

Classroom links

Discuss with the children the people or rules they think they should obey.

See Infant Handbook for a topic on Eid ul-Fitr, the festival which marks the end of Ramadan.

Eid ul-Fitr
– Follow up Assembly

Purpose

To mark a festival which is important to many people in this country and for children to value the presence of different festivals in this country.

Eid-ul-Fitr is the celebration that marks the end of Ramadan. Muslims give thanks that the month is over, and they give to the poor so that everyone can join in the celebrations. Often new clothes are bought, and there are parties in the home. Figs (and fig rolls), dates and other sweet fruits are popular. It is also a time of reconciliation.

Preparation

Cut fig rolls into slices or quarters, enough for every child to have a bit if they want some.

Make an enormous Eid card with the words, "We wish you a Happy Eid" large enough for all the children to read.

(You could copy a commercial one or simply make a card with flowers on the front – no pictures of people or animals.)

Remind the children about Ramadan and tell them that the new moon has come and therefore the month has now ended. Ask them how they think Muslim people must be feeling.

Tell them how they have parties to celebrate (you could mention that there is no alcohol because it is forbidden in Islam).

Tell them about the celebrations, giving particular attention to the practice of giving to the poor so that they have enough money or food to celebrate the festival too.

Pass round the pieces of fig roll explaining that figs are very popular with the Muslims who come from the hot dry countries where figs and dates grow.

Ask children to send a Happy Eid greeting to all Muslims by saying "We wish you a Happy Eid" all together in a very loud voice.

Or teach them the Arabic phrase "Eid Mubarak", which means the same thing.

HALLOWEEN

Concern has been expressed about the treatment of Halloween in schools. These two assemblies are designed to address the deeper significance of a very popular festival, without encouraging interest in the occult, or being 'scary' for its own sake.

1. The Witch's Brew

Resources
A 'witch's cauldron' which could be made from a plastic bucket with black paper gathered round the outside.

Pictures or objects to symbolise different sorts of unpleasantness or evil in the world, for example a toy gun for people fighting, a torn toy animal for cruelty to animals, an empty wooden bowl for hunger. Others to show things you or the children might be afraid of: a picture of a spider or slug, perhaps.

Leader:
There are many times when things go wrong. There are times when people hurt our feelings, there are times when we hurt other people. There are times when we try to do something good and it all goes wrong. There are times when we are angry with people, and times when people are angry with us.

All these things give us bad feelings inside. Usually we keep them inside and we don't like to talk about bad feelings very much. Halloween is a time when we can let out our bad feelings and think about them. It can be frightening to think about bad things, so we have fun and jokes at Halloween to help us be brave enough to think about the bad things. We make ugly masks and pictures of monsters, and we play with them. Perhaps we are trying to learn that it is all right to be frightened sometimes.

What we are going to do this morning is make a spell. We are going to put all sorts of nasty things into my witch's cauldron.

Introduce each picture or object, talk about it, and put it in the cauldron, with some simple phrase to show what is symbolises, for example:
We hurt each other.
We feel upset because someone has hurt us.
We get angry.
We are often frightened.
We are sometimes jealous of other people, etc.

Ask the children to mime each of these emotions as you talk about them – but without touching anyone else.

Stir the cauldron and ask the children what kind of spell it would make. Would they want anyone to cast that spell on them? Perhaps they could mime the effect of the spell – again without touching anyone else.
Leader: So let's cook what is in this cauldron and try to make a spell that makes things better. Let us say these words as I stir the pot.

Prayer/reflection
Sometimes we hurt people – we don't want to.
Sometimes people hurt us – we don't want them to.
Sometimes we are angry – we don't want to be.
Sometimes we are frightened – we don't want to be.
Sometimes we are jealous – we don't want to be.
All our bad things are in the cauldron.
We'll stir them and cook them
And tell them in chorus:
'We don't want you – don't come back!'

May we have good thoughts to save us from our bad thoughts, today and everyday.

Song
Come and Praise 50 When a Knight won his spurs

2. Things we are Frightened of

Resources

A black 'halloween' spider and a picture of the patterns on a real spider (Pictorial Charts Educational Trust publish one in their set W737 Symmetry in Nature – obtainable from 27 Kirchen Road, London W13 OUD)

A 'halloween' skeleton and a proper scientific diagram of a skeleton, or an x-ray photograph.

Talk about Halloween, and how people play with frightening things at Halloween.

Leader: There are always things we are frightened of. Some of them are sensible things to be frightened of. I myself am frightened of … [something like crossing a busy road, walking too near a cliff edge]. But there are also things people are frightened of for no reason. It doesn't make any difference to say there is no danger, they are just frightened. I myself am frightened of … [something like spiders, slugs, dark corners]. Halloween helps us admit that we are frightened. It can also help us look at the things that frighten us. And sometimes, when you look at something carefully, it is not as frightening as you first thought.

In this bag I have a toy spider. It looks rather nasty and scary. I'm going to take it out. If you are frightened of spiders, shut your eyes now, and open them when you feel brave enough.

Take out the spider and talk a bit about it, let one or two children play with it if they want (at the front, where they cannot torment a child who is frightened of it.) The aim is to give children time to open their eyes if they had shut them.

But this is nothing like a real spider. Let's have a look at a picture of a real spider, and see if that is frightening. Again, you can shut your eyes now if you want to.

Talk about the picture of the spider, the patterns on its body, the shape of its legs, etc.

Alternatively, go through a similar exercise with the skeleton. With the picture of the real thing, talk about how bones keep our body in shape, how intricately they link together, how strong they are.

Prayer/reflection

There are many things in the world that we do not like.

There are many things in the world that frighten us.

At Halloween we try to look at some of these things. We try to find ways of not being frightened.

From ghoulies and ghosties and long-leggedy beasties
And things that go bump in the night
Good Lord, deliver us.

Song

Come and praise 44 He who would valiant be (The words of this are difficult for infants, but children often like it, and some ideas are conveyed even if they do not understand much of it.)

LENT

If Lent co-incides with Ramadan the assemblies for each could be adapted accordingly.

Purpose
The objective of this assembly is to draw attention to the notion of feasting and fasting.

Resources
Various items or pictures associated with different times of the year, e.g autumn leaves, pictures of snow, bucket and spade etc.

Show children the items or pictures (see list above) and ask them what time of the year they associate with it – encourage them to think of other things they associate with that season.

Then go on to say that many Christians have another way of naming the parts of the year – they call them the church seasons. Just as we think of certain things we like to do with the seasons of spring, summer, winter and autumn, so do Christians with their church seasons.

Ask the children to suggest what might be associated with the season of Christmas – what would people be thinking about then?

See if they can remember back to the time or season of Advent.

And what about the season of Easter – what do the children associate with that?

Tell them that it is now the season of Lent. It is the period when Christians remember Jesus growing up and becoming a man. They remember how he decided to go about the countryside preaching about God's love and forgiveness. He knew that he would have to leave his home and give up many of the things he liked. Perhaps it was his mother's cooking. Perhaps it was the happiness of sawing wood with his father, Joseph. Perhaps it was seeing his friends in the village.

He decided too that for a time he would give up being with other people and having fun. He was a person who enjoyed having fun and laughter with other people. Before he started teaching people he wanted time to think and get ready. So he went out into the stony desert to pray. For forty days he didn't think about the needs of his body, about food or drink. He thought only about what he believed God wanted him to do. At the end he came back to the villages and began to teach.

So now many Christians have a season of the year when they remember Jesus in the desert . It's not a happy, exciting season like Christmas or Easter. Instead it's a quiet time when they meet together to study their holy book, the Bible, or think about what it means to be a Christian. Many Christians also decide to give up something which they really like during Lent – often it is sweets and sweet food. In the past, everyone used to use up all the sugar in the house on the day before Lent started. One way of doing this was by eating pancakes: that is how pancake day started.

Ask the children to suggest what colours they think would go with the season of Lent.

Prayer/reflection
Ask for a period of silence in which the children are asked to think about being alone. Ask them to close their eyes and imagine that they are all alone. Then open them and be glad that there are friends around them.

Classroom links
There is a topic on Lent/Easter in the REAL Infant Handbook which looks at the life of Jesus.

Are there times when the children like being by themselves in a room if they know there is someone else in the house? Discuss this further.

Follow-up Assemblies
This is a time to use the parables of Jesus as assembly topics. (See *A Tapestry of Tales*.)

AN EASTER LITURGY

Preparation

A table at the front, as plain in shape and colour as possible, with nothing on it. No pictures or flowers in the hall. Make the whole hall as bare and bleak as possible.

Each class to prepare a symbol of spring and new life, with words and/or songs to go with it.

Have ready pictures and streamers to decorate the hall at the end.

Leader: 2,000 years ago on Good Friday
Jesus was taken to die,
on a cross, on a hill.
His friends were weeping,
in their hearts it felt like the cold, bleak winter.
Life seemed without hope.

So today we start our Easter service with the table bare, as the world is bare in winter. Nothing is on it. It is empty and clear.

Hymm: a quiet, reflective one. eg. Kum ba yah

Leader: The friends of Jesus took the body and laid it in a tomb, an open cave on the hillside. They rolled a big rock in front of it. For two days they grieved for him. But then the Bible tells us that on the third day they found the tomb empty. Jesus, instead of being dead and gone, was alive, standing among them. His friends announced it to the world. "Jesus is risen, Jesus is alive!"

Now their hearts no longer felt like winter. Suddenly it felt like spring. Now they had hope that there was new life.

So at Easter we remember the story of Jesus rising from the dead and we think of new life beginning all around us in the spring. We remember that when things seem bad, good will come again. We remember that when things seem dead, life will come again. We remember that when things are cold, warmth will come again.

Invite a child from each class to come forward with a symbol of spring, and talk briefly about how it shows new life and changes. Alternatively the class could sing a short song about the item. For example:

daffodils – show how the bulbs are buried in the ground and look dead, but the plant grows from them and flowers.

eggs – an egg looks dead, but when the mother bird sits on it and keeps it warm, new life comes out of it. Coloured or decorated Easter eggs could also be used with a note of their connection with new life at Easter.

a twig with buds – a dead looking twig will soon burst into leaf.

frogspawn – a dead looking jelly will soon hatch into living tadpoles.

seeds, e.g. bean seeds – as for daffodils above.

an animal hibernating, e.g. tortoise just waking from hibernation – the animal is asleep and looks dead, but will soon wake up again.

Each item is placed on the table, to build up a spring display of new life.

Leader: When we began today, our table was barren and bare.
Now it is full of symbols of new life:
Plants that grow again,
Animals that live again,
Newborn creatures springing to life.
After winter, life starts again.
After we have been terribly sad, happiness can come again.

We remember the friends of Jesus.
We remember how they told the world,
'Jesus is risen from the dead!'
And we give thanks for the Spring and for new life
and hope.

Children: Amen

Hymn: Come and Praise 130 All in an Easter
Garden

131 Now the Green
Blade Rises

During the singing, some teachers and children
could go round putting up pictures on the bare
walls, perhaps adding short streamers in spring
colours, to give a festive air to the hall.

AN ADVENT LITURGY

There is a growing tendency to ignore the season of Advent and start celebrating Christmas in November. Obviously, the school's Christmas celebration has to be before Christmas itself, but we suggest you make this as late as possible, and concentrate instead on creating an atmosphere of expectation, waiting and preparation. This Advent liturgy is designed to help with this.

Resources

A large postbox, could be cardboard, with times of collection and delivery on it. If you regularly have a postbox this could be changed by decking it with holly.

Large figures of Mary and Joseph and possibly a donkey. These could be painted on to thick durable card or made out of cardboard tubes.

A large candle marked off at intervals according to the number of assemblies you will have in the season.

The theme of light at Christmas is taken up again in the REAL Junior Handbook and Assembly Book.

Preparing for Christmas

Tell children that Advent which began or will begin on Sunday is a time of preparation for Christmas, though some people start much earlier. So today in assembly we are putting things around the hall to help everyone prepare for Christmas.

1) Two children or an adult come forward carrying the postbox. Comment on how Christmas is a time that people wish each other peace and a happy time. One way of doing this is by sending cards. Look at the collection and delivery times painted on the box and set it in its position for the next few weeks.

Prayer/reflection

We wish peace and happiness to our friends at Christmas.

We wish peace and happiness to strangers at Christmas.

In Advent we prepare. In Advent we get ready.

Let us prepare peace. Let us make happiness ready.

We are waiting for Christmas to come.

2) A child comes forward with the figures or a painting of Mary and Joseph. Comment on how at this time Christians think of Mary and Joseph setting off for Bethlehem, not really knowing what lay ahead of them. Looking at the pictures reminds us that at Christmas time there is a story of Jesus and his birth, not just the fun of a party in the middle of winter.

Prayer/reflection

Mary and Joseph set out.

The times were hard, the journey was long.

No-one was ready to welcome them.

No-one was ready to take them in.

They waited for their baby to be born,

And people are waiting for Christmas to come.

3) A child comes forward carrying the Advent candle. Light it and tell the children how candles are lit at Christmas because Christians think of Jesus coming as a light to a world that was dark.

Prayer/reflection

One candle shines today.

One candle says, 'Prepare!'

Many things to get ready,

Christmas means many things.

At Christmas hundreds of candles shine,

But one candle shines today,

For people are waiting for Christmas to come.

Sing a carol already known to the children.

Mary and Joseph's Journey – Follow up Assembly

In Mexico it is the custom for the figures of Mary and Joseph to be moved from house to house each night as though going on a journey. Similarly you could make a small ritual of moving the figures of Mary and Joseph with each assembly during the Christmas season. In a hall with classrooms lead-ing off it the children could find a "lodging" outside each one. Each class could fashion its own house. As part of the final Christmas assembly they could arrive in Bethlehem.

The advent candle could be lit to burn during the intervening assemblies whether they be news times, class assemblies, or carol practices.

Classroom links

There is a topic on Christmas in the REAL Infant Handbook. The Advent calendar described there could be adapted for use in assembly.

A CHRISTMAS LITURGY

This assembly or service is based on the idea of the candlelit service of 9 lessons and carols held in many churches.

Preparation

Preparation of the children's accounts of the story needs to be done in the classroom – these could be the results of group work preceded by extemporary dramatizing of the stories.

While the children who have specific roles may need to be rehearsed, the others should not be, except to practise carols. We are suggesting not a performance, but a service which may be an alternative to the nativity play for parents.

The children sit in a circle, leaving five evenly spaced gaps. One gap is filled with a table set out with a stable bare of anything but a few animals. Above this is the advent candle. Readers are positioned at each of the other four gaps, with a teacher to hold a large candle for reading.

It might be better for the children to remain seated for the carols to maintain an atmosphere of peace.

The hall should be as dimly lit as possible.

Any carols which the children enjoy would be suitable, especially those which tell all or part of the Christmas story. Two suggestions from Come and Praise: 121 The Virgin Mary had a Baby Boy, and 123 Mary had a Baby. There are four 'slots' for carols in the suggested liturgy. One or two carols could be split between them, a verse or two at a time, or repeated at different points.

Resources

Advent candle, chime bars, glockenspiel and handbells. Figures of Mary, Joseph, shepherds and wise men (alternatively children could be dressed in these roles and move forward to form a tableau).

The leader gives a brief introduction to the format and asks the children to sit in absolute silence while the advent candle is lit for the last time.

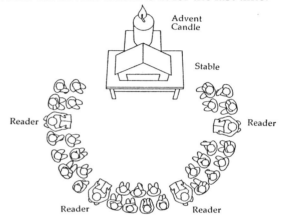

Chime bars, glockenspiel or handbells play short simple chords.

During the playing the advent candle is lit.

1st reading: Child's account of the annunciation to Mary.

Carol.

2nd reading: Child's account of the journey to Bethlehem and the birth in the stable.

Two children bring forward the figures of Mary and Joseph and place them in the stable.

Another child comes from a different direction and places the baby in the crib.

Carol.

3rd reading: Child's account of the angel's appearance to the shepherds.

Children bring figures of shepherds and sheep and place them by the crib.

Carol.

4th reading: Child's account of the wise men.

Children bring the figures of the wise men and place them by the crib.

Carol.

Leader: A blessing or a prayer.

Mary had her baby in the quiet and darkness of the stable: may we have times of quiet, peaceful happiness this Christmas.

The shepherds heard the angel's singing fill the heavens: may we have times of loud, joyful happiness this Christmas.

The wise men brought gifts to the baby Jesus: may we share the happiness of giving this Christmas.

And may God's blessing be on all of us as we celebrate this happy time.
Silence.

A tune is played on the chime bars as the four candle bearers move forward and move in procession out of the door.

SHARING THE HARVEST

Harvest is a recurring theme in Jewish and Hindu festivals with the harvests of different crops being celebrated at different times. In the Christian calendar it is a 19th century innovation and is traditionally a thanks for cereal crops and fruit though it is not confined to this.

In the REAL Junior Handbook harvest is celebrated as a festival for the environment.

Preparation

Each class prepares some food to contribute to the harvest so that the children as well as their parents are giving something. We suggest the following to represent a variety of food. Some could be made ahead and if necessary frozen to avoid pressure on use of the school oven, though not all involve cooking:

glazed bread or bread rolls- a traditional harvest sheaf with a mouse on it would need expert adult input but would tie in with the theme of sharing harvest with the animals.

chocolate crackles – remind children that the cereal involved is rice.

fruit jellies

biscuits cut in animal shapes

peppermint creams

a light fruit cake

chapattis

potato cakes

seed cake for birds.

Prepare a harvest display, possibly including rangoli patterns: see the topic on 'Pattern' in the REAL Infant Handbook. There the emphasis is on the patterning. Here it is on the different foodstuffs. Make the patterns by sticking grain, pulses, pasta etc. to paper circles.

Begin with a Hymn such as any from Come and Praise pp133-139.

Leader: Today at Harvest festival we give thanks for food. Not just the food which is piled before us here but the food we eat every day.

We are blessed with food – it helps to keep us healthy.

We are blessed with food – we can enjoy its taste.

We give thanks for those who grow and harvest it.

Children: Amen

Leader: We give thanks for those who transport and sell it.

Children: Amen

Leader: We give thanks for those who prepare and cook it.

Children: Amen

Leader: One important way of giving thanks for food is by sharing it with others.

The children have brought food from home to share with others in the community.

They have also made food themselves to share with others.

Representatives from different classes come forward in turn to offer food, each one saying a little bit about what they have made, or singing a relevant song.

Leader: The food before us we will share with other people but we must not forget the others who live in our community, the animals and birds. At the Hindu harvest festival of Divali people in India often decorate the steps of the house with food put out for the animals. (If the children have made rangoli patterns draw attention to them.) Today the children have brought and made food for animals as well.

Children bring food for animals, saying a little bit about what they have done.

Song
Any harvest hymn, or Come and Praise 79, 'From the tiny ant'.

Classroom links
Science targets on energy and heat, in cooking. Food and health and knowledge of plants and growth.

REMEMBRANCE DAY

The Remembrance Day assembly is a short self-contained rite. First we give two focuses for assemblies in preparation for it. There are assemblies on the same theme in the REAL Junior Assembly Book. The two Remembrance Day services could be combined and modified to make an assembly for a whole primary school.

The Poppies of Remembrance – Assembly Focus

This assembly could be held a couple of weeks before 11th November when the poppies are already on sale.

Purpose
To begin to convey to children the sorrow that war brings. To explain the meaning of the red poppy and to prepare for the Remembrance Day assembly.

Resources
Some remembrance poppies, and possibly a single large paper or silk red poppy, a picture or pictures of First World War service men and women and equipment.

(6 mins)
Lots of children enjoy playing at being soldiers and shooting one another. The big toy shops know this because they sell toy guns and machine guns and tanks and action men in combat gear. Some children want to be soldiers when they are grown up and of course some men and women do join the army, navy or air force when they grow up. But most of them do other jobs like being bus-

drivers, teachers, post office workers, doctors or building cars in factories. Nowadays although there are still some soldiers, most people have other jobs and they don't think about wars and armies except when they see the news on television.

It was very different about 80 years ago. In 1914 everybody in the country was thinking about war because this country, Britain, was fighting the country of Germany. Lots and lots of the young men said that they would go and fight in the war. They would go and fight for their country. Other men said that they didn't believe in killing people but they would go and help by looking after people who got sick and were wounded. Young women didn't go to fight but they became nurses so they too could help look after the injured. In the factories they stopped making ordinary things like pots and pans and bicycles and everyone worked at making guns and ammunition. Women who had always worked at home went to work in factories, or driving buses and doing jobs that men had always done until then. Old ladies and mothers with young children helped by knitting socks for the soldiers.

When the soldiers first went to fight they sang songs and told jokes. When they sat on the boats crossing over to France and Belgium, where the battles were being fought, they felt very excited and were looking forward to the adventure that lay ahead. They would defend their country. They would be heroes.

But they soon found it wasn't like that at all. Much of the war was fought in big fields. The soldiers would rush forward towards the enemy, firing their guns. Sometimes they took a little bit of land from the enemy. Then the soldiers dug deep ditches on the land and lived in them to stop the enemy soldiers coming and taking the land again. Sometimes they sat in the ditches which they had captured from the enemy soldiers. These deep ditches are usually called trenches. Most of the time it was very boring. The soldiers were cold. They were hungry and the food was not very good to eat. Their boots leaked, their clothes were always damp. Lots of men died in the fighting and lots of men died because they got sick.

Yes, many of them were very brave and many were heroes. There are stories of men who risked their own lives to rescue a friend who lay wounded on the battlefield. Instead of running back as fast as they could because there were bullets flying all around them, they had to go slowly because they were dragging or carrying a wounded man.

And the fields where they were fighting stopped being green and pleasant. They became churned up, and turned into slushy, horrible mud.

In the end the war was won. It took four long years. Children who were babies when their dads went to war were starting school when they came back for good. Children who were just five when the war started were in the junior school when it ended.

And lots of the men never came back because they had died on the battlefield. Some of them had children, and now those children had no fathers. Many of them had wives, and now those wives had no husbands. Lots of the men who came back were sick or had wounds from which they would never fully recover. There were some who had lost both legs and could not walk, some had lost their eyesight, and some had lost an arm or a hand. All of them had lost friends who had died, and all of them were very different from the happy young men who had set off to war. Normal life began again in Britain but it was different from how it had been before.

And in the fields where the battles had been fought, life started again. The first flowers that sprung up across the fields were bright red poppies, hundreds and hundreds of them. People looking at them said that the red looked like the blood of the dead and wounded, but the flowers also were a sign of hope, as the dead mud of the fields came back to life. People said they would never forget the sight of the fields full of poppies.

In Britain people didn't want to forget the men who had died and they wanted to help their widows and children and the men who were injured. So they started to sell paper poppies to raise money and to help people remember those who had died. Today poppies are still sold. Not many people are alive from that great and terrible war which is called the First World War, but the money goes to help those who have been hurt by other wars since then.

Prayer/reflection
Silence
The red poppies remind us that people are hurt by war and fighting. Let's try to be adults and children who live peacefully together.

Classroom links
Discuss with the children why they think children fight with one another.

Make pictures of poppies or fields with poppies in them to put in the assembly hall for Remembrance Day (paper collages would be effective).

Signs of Peace – Assembly Focus

Purpose
The objective is to encourage the idea that peace is of value and to identify the dove as a symbol of peace.

Resources
Pictures of a lion, a mule, an elephant, a fox and a dove; a painting showing the Holy Spirit as a dove – 'The baptism of Jesus' by Piero della Francesca in the National Gallery is a very clear one.

Look at pictures of different animals and talk briefly and humorously about sayings associated with them:
e.g. as brave as a lion
as stubborn as a mule
a memory like an elephant
as cunning as a fox
as busy as a bee

Then look at 'as peaceful as doves'. Tell the children that doves have been a symbol of peace for hundreds and hundreds of years and that often when artists wanted to paint God's spirit they painted it as a white dove because God wants peace for people.

Prayer/reflection
Leader: The doves remind us of peace. Let us be adults and children who live peacefully together.

Children: Amen

Songs
Come and Praise 143 I've got peace like a river;
                    144 Peace is flowing;
                    149 The Vine and the Fig tree.
Alleluya   42 Let There be Peace on
                     Earth

Classroom links

Make simple paper doves, as many as possible, to hang on string in the assembly hall.

In a dance class children can make up simple dances to appropiate music about the different animals from the assembly – or simply a dove dance.

Make up simple stories about peace, e.g. 'I feel peaceful when....'

or 'It is peaceful when....'

In drama children working in pairs can make up a simple story of two children quarrelling and making friends again.

Remembrance Day
– Assembly Focus

Purpose

The purpose of this assembly is to share in the Act of Remembrance.

Note: Originally the Act of Remembrance was held on November 11th at 11 o'clock (see below). It has now been moved to the nearest Sunday. In school it is appropriate to revert to the original date and time if possible.

Preparation

Fill the assembly hall with the children's pictures of poppies and with the doves and perhaps any stories the children have written.

Have a table covered with a red or white tablecloth and set with a large candle.

Have four children ready with bunches of home-made paper poppies or real flowers.

Start comfortably before 11 o'clock.

Play quiet solemn music as the children come in and sit down.

Tell the children that the peace agreement after the First World War was signed at 11 o'clock, on the 11th day of November which is the eleventh month of the year. For many years two minutes silence was kept on that day at that time to remember those who had died. This is what we shall be doing today, the 11th November. Nowadays the date is changed to a Sunday.

Comment on the poppies and doves in the hall.

Sing one of the songs suggested above, or
Alleluya 45 Last Night I had the Strangest
       Dream;
      46 Peace will soon come to be.

Leader (adult or child): Today we remember soldiers who have died in wars.
Child lays one of the bunches of flowers.
Leader: Today we remember the doctors and nurses who have died in wars.
Child lays another bunch of flowers.
Leader: Today we remember those who refused to fight but died helping rescue the injured in war.
Child lays another bunch of flowers.
Leader: Today we remember the children who have died or been hurt as a result of war.
Child lays another bunch of flowers.
Leader: Now we will light this candle of remembrance and at the 11th hour of the 11th day of the 11th month we will stand in silence to remember the dead of all wars.
Light candle, followed by a minute (or half a minute's) silence.
Leader: Today we have remembered those who have died as a result of war. Let us be adults and children who live peacefully together.
Sing a hymn and walk out to quiet music.

Classroom links

Look at the greetings that people use that mean 'peace':

Hebrew *shalom alechem*, Arabic *Salaam aleikum*.

AN ASSEMBLY FOR ELECTION TIME

Purpose
What makes a good leader?

Preparation
This story is particularly appropriate for election times and could be introduced with a reference to the election, especially if polling is taking place within the school. Children can be given a simple account of the responsibilities of those elected, whether it is to allocate money for local needs, or to make laws and distribute national taxes.

The story could also be used more generally at other times.

Resources
Display pictures of the candidates.

(2 mins)
This story comes from the Jewish tradition.

Long, long ago Moses was a shepherd in the land of Midian. All day he watched over his flocks with tender care. Other shepherds let their sheep race for the grass – the older, stronger ones would push the younger ones out of the way – and the shepherds didn't care. But Moses was not like this. He always led the young weak sheep out to graze first so that they could build up their strength. Next he led the slightly older sheep to nibble the herbs that were good for them. Finally he let the impatient older ones out to chew at the hard grass.

Once a young lamb escaped from the flock. Moses saw it go out of the corner of his eye.

"You naughty rascal," he said to himself, "Where are you off to?"

Many a shepherd would have let the lamb go its own way, for what is one lamb among many? Other shepherds might have gone after the lamb but they would have given it a good beating to teach it a lesson. But not Moses.

He called to his son to look after the flock and off he went; scrambling over rocks, scratching himself on thorny bushes as he chased the lamb. Then at last it stopped by a stream, panting. Moses stopped and he too was panting but he was not angry.

"Ah, poor lamb!" he said, "I didn't know you were thirsty." He let the lamb drink, then he gently picked up the trembling creature and carried it back to the rest of his flock.

God in heaven looked down at Moses and saw how he cared for his sheep. He saw how he treated each one according to its needs. And God said:

"I want someone to look after the people of Israel. I want someone who will treat them with tenderness. A man who looks after his sheep so lovingly, will surely be a man to care for people."

So God chose Moses to look after his people because he knew that Moses would care for the young and the weak among them.

Prayer/reflection
Tomorrow adults throughout the city/country will be choosing men and women to be on the council or in parliament. May they choose wisely. May they choose men and women who will truly care for the people of this city/county . People who will be concerned for the weak and the needy and the young, as Moses was concerned for the weak among his sheep.

A New Leader
– Follow up Assembly

The leader tells the children the name of the person elected, shows them his/her picture, and reminds them of his or her responsibilities. (Party politics need never be mentioned.)

Before taking part in any debates in the House of Commons, each MP must swear an oath or make a solemn affirmation that they will loyally serve the Queen. You could discuss with the children why this means doing their best for everyone in the country.

Prayer/reflection

Give wisdom to .... and all others elected yesterday. Help them as they make decisions. May they be like Moses the shepherd and think about the needs of the weak and the poor.

Songs

Explain to the children that the songs below express some of what a new councillor or MP might (or should) be thinking.

Come and Praise 47 One more step along the world
50 When a Knight won his spurs
68 Kum ba yah
71 If I had a hammer

THE DEATH OF A SCHOOL PET

Purpose

The aim is to remember and commemorate collectively the life of a school pet. It is often said that the death of a pet may be a child's first experience of bereavement and can be an opportunity for learning about death. However the death of a classroom pet is frequently passed over as quickly as possible by teachers, perhaps because it is painful for them as well. Children in other classes may also feel sad about it and yet may hear of the death only by rumour. Pets often stay with the teacher rather than with the particular group of children, and therefore may have been known by more than one class of children. Siblings sometimes grow fond of the pet when they visit the classroom or it comes home for the weekend. So the death of a class pet is also an event for the whole school.

Rituals can have an important role to play in coming to terms with loss, whether it be a simple burial service for a goldfish in the back yard, or funeral rites for a person. A school 'memorial' assembly gives the opportunity for a communal acknowledgement of what the animal meant to the children. However, we present it not as a full assembly but rather as the focus for a more general assembly in order to differentiate it from the tragic event of the death of a child or adult associated with the school, when a qualitatively different sort of service in school would be appropriate.

Preparation

Children, teachers and parents who have known the animal are asked to contribute to a memorial book for it. Subjects could include: how it got its name, how it came to the school, its behaviour during the school day, its escape efforts, taking it home for the weekend, how they felt about its death. The aim is to be positive about the life of the pet.

You'll need to make sure that all classes are told of the death beforehand so that it doesn't come as a shock in assembly.

Remembering Our Pet – Assembly Focus

Remind children of the death of the animal and how many in the school felt sad at the news.

Read extracts from the memorial book yourself, or ask the contributors to read, or a mixture of both.

Prayer/reflection

Leader: We give thanks for the life of … and the joy he/she gave many of us.
Children: Amen

THE BIRTH OF A BABY

From time to time the school will wish to celebrate the birth of a baby in whom they have a special interest – the child of a member of staff, perhaps a royal baby, or the brother or sister of a child in the school. The assembly will have more meaning if the children have to some extent followed the course of the pregnancy, and if the baby can be present for the assembly, but this is not necessary. From time to time you might decide to celebrate all the babies connected with the school who have been born in, say, the last six months. You could invite them all in for the assembly, if your nerves can stand it! The infant topic on 'Babies' in the REAL Infant Handbook would be a good one to teach here, and some of the ideas for the assembly are drawn from the topic.

Preparation

The teacher needs to arrange for a baby or babies to be present if possible.

In the classroom prepare 'wishes' for the baby (see below), as paintings, models, or plays.

One child should be prepared to sum up the wishes.

Resources

As introduction or closing, you could use some of the 'cradle music' available on record. For example Wagner's 'Siegfried Idyll' was written for the first birthday of his son, which was the same day as his wife's birthday. He had it played outside her window.

Leader: Today we welcome baby ____. A new life. A new joy for her mother and father, and a new responsibility for them. As she grows up, they will need to give her the right kind of food, they will need to keep her warm, and they will need to keep her safe from dangers. Most important of all, she will need their love.

I wonder what sort of a person she will be? Will she be noisy or quiet, will she like sports, will she be a good singer? No doubt her mother and father have their own ideas about what they want for her as she grows.

Parents have different ways of showing their wishes for their baby. Sometimes they buy special presents, or encourage their baby to do one thing rather than another. When a mother is expecting her baby and it is still inside her, she sometimes plays music so that the baby can hear it and be soothed by it, and come to love music. Many Hindu mothers read from their holy book to the baby inside them, so that it will always love the holy book. When the baby is born, Hindu mothers often make sure that the first taste of solid food is something sweet. This is a way of saying, "We wish our baby to have a sweet and happy life." What will this baby have as her first solid food? (Ask mother, or get suggestions from children.)

Do you remember the story of Sleeping Beauty? When the princess was born, twelve good fairies brought gifts to the baby. One gave her beauty, one gave her a good temper, another gave her the ability to sing like a bird, and so on. We are not fairies, and we cannot make our wishes for baby ____ come true, but class ____ have thought what wishes they have for her, and have prepared some fairy gifts. See if you can guess what each one is wishing for her.

Children bring paintings or models which symbolise different good wishes for the baby in her future life. The rest of the school can play a guessing game to find out what each one signifies.

Then a child can sum up all the wishes:
Baby ____, we wish you
good health,
many friends,

wise and understanding parents,
the love of those around you,
_____ etc.

If the school has collected for a gift for the baby, it could be presented at this point.

Prayer/reflection

Father in Heaven, bless the parents of _____, that they may love and look after their child; make them wise and understanding, to help (him) as (he) grows, and surround (his) family with the light of truth and the warmth of love. Amen.

You could bless the child, using the words from Numbers, chapter 6, verse 23-26.

Note: anyone can pronounce a blessing on others; it is not a priest's prerogative. The Jewish Sabbath celebrations include the father blessing his children using these same words:

'May the Lord bless you and keep you.
May the Lord let his face shine on you and be gracious to you.
May the Lord look kindly on you and give you peace.'

Or learn some of the 'Sabbath Prayer' from *Fiddler on the Roof.*

Songs

Come and Praise 19 He's got the whole world in his hands including the line, 'He's got the tiny little baby...'.

WELCOME – THE START OF A NEW SCHOOL YEAR

Purpose
To welcome new members of the school and to give children a sense of school identity in starting the new year.

Preparation
Make a large welcome sign.

If there are children or staff whose first language is not English find out how to say and write welcome in their language. Add greetings in different languages.

For example:
Bienvenue	French
Salaam Aleikum	Arabic
Karibuni	Swahili
Croeso	Welsh

Children could play a part in the introductions if there is sufficient time before the assembly to prepare it.

Welcome

Leader: Tell the children that today we are welcoming new people to the school. Greet them generally with welcome in appropriate languages (see above).

Introduce new members of staff (including ancillary staff), saying a little bit about each one.

Ask the children to clap to show they are pleased to have them in the school.

Then welcome the new children in the school, the new class that has joined, and any new children who have started that year.

Again ask the children to clap.

Then briefly talk about what it means to make people feel welcome, e.g. showing them the way around the school, being friendly and polite, helping them if they don't understand something.

Perhaps talk about any experience you may have had of feeling lost or strange in a new situation.

Finally talk about welcoming the new school year and the opportunity it brings to make new friends, see old ones and learn new things.

Prayer/reflection
We start a new year.
We do not know what people we shall meet.
We do not know what new things we shall learn.
We do not know what will happen.
Let us set out on the adventure of the new year.
Let us greet the new year with gladness.

Welcome the new year with clapping and/or ask the children to shake hands with the people on either side of them to wish them well for the coming year. (The youngest children might find this difficult).

Songs
Come and Praise 87 Give us Hope Lord for Each Day
Note: At future assemblies make any new people in the school feel welcome in a similar way.

THE END OF THE SCHOOL YEAR – SAYING GOODBYE

Purpose

The end of the school year inevitably brings some farewells as children move on to a new class or to another school, and members of staff may leave. In religious practice the end of the year is a time of accounting, adding up the financial and the spiritual books. In school it can be a time of giving a report on the school.

Preparations

Ask the children to prepare a list of happy things which have happened during the year at school; you also need another list of sad events; a list of all the people who are leaving.

Leader: It is the end of the school year so it is a time of remembering and of saying goodbye.

1st child reads a list of happy things that have happened during the year.

Everyone either cheers or claps the good things of the year.

2nd child reads a list of anything sad that has happened during the year.

Keep a time of brief silence.

If the list is empty ask the children to be quiet to remember that some individuals may have experienced sadness during the year.

Leader: Today is sad in some ways because it is a time of saying good-bye. Go through the list of people leaving.

Possibly give sweets to all those leaving, with the words:

"We give you a sweet now because we wish you a sweet time in everything you do".

Prayer/reflection

You could use this blessing, either said or sung:
May the long time sun shine upon you
All love surround you
And the true light within you
Guide you all the way home.

Songs

Come and Praise 141 Shalom
Alleluya   49 Hevenu Shalom

CROSS-REFERENCE TABLE

Use this table to find links between assemblies in this book and the topics in the REAL Infant Handbook.

Assemblies	Babies	Houses and Homes	Clothing	Food	Family	Myself	Colour	People	The Wind and Weather	Toys and Treasures	Time	Pattern	Pets	Birthdays	Buildings	Shops	The Senses	Easter	Chinese New Year	Eid ul-Fitr	Christmas
Celebrating The Person			•			•		•						•							
The School Community				•				•			•				•						
Tiddalik the Bullfrog						•															
The Wise Teacher								•													
Happy Memories				•		•		•			•										
The Monkey Bridge				•		•		•													
Karen's Tree																					
Being Detectives		•							•					•							
Good But Can Harm Us																					
Fire																					
Rain																					
Short But Sweet			•						•			•									
We Are All Different				•		•		•				•									
In The Dark						•															
Blessings			•														•				
Old But Valued										•											
Stewardship										•			•								
Being Alone						•															
How Should You Judge…		•					•														
Saint Kevin													•								
What Makes Life …			•																		
Mother Love	•		•	•				•													
Akbar		•	•																		
Saying Amen																					
Divali			•	•			•									•					
Chinese New Year			•	•			•									•			•		
Ramadan/Eid			•									•				•				•	
Halloween						•	•									•					
Lent/Easter			•				•									•		•			
Advent/Christmas			•	•			•							•		•					•
Sharing the Harvest			•				•									•					
Remembrance Day																					
Election Time								•													
Death of a School Pet													•								
The Birth of a Baby	•				•																
Start/End of School Year																•					